PRAISE FOR *FRESH START*

"I think Doug is the best communicator of our day. And in *Fresh Start* he provides a way for the most stuck and stagnant person to pick up their mat and not walk, or run, but fly. This book is what God's unleashing truth is all about, and no one says it better than Doug."

STEVE ARTERBURN
Host of "New Life Live"
Best-selling author of *Regret-Free Living*

"Sometimes it's easy to forget that we have a limited amount of time in this life. We could keep sitting on our unconfronted pain, anger, and bad habits indefinitely, letting them sap away our time and strength, *or* we can let God deal with them and give us a new, fresh start. In *Fresh Start*, Doug puts his finger on those things we're "living with" and doesn't let up until we truly understand where it all came from and how God is eager to deliver us. It's the perfect jumpstart to the process of letting go—and letting God set us free."

KERRY SHOOK
Sr. Pastor, Woodlands Church
Best-selling author of *One Month to Live*

"Doug Fields has written a wonderful book! He takes the truth of dedication and puts it into easy language, gives us practical tools, and motivates us to truly become all God calls us to be. *This* is a book that excites me!"

SUSIE SHELLENBERGER
Editor, SUSIE Magazine

"Fields' book provides some great biblical insights combined with excellent life skills. Anyone interested in making a difference in the world should read it! It's a recipe for a life of significance."

RICK JOHNSON
Author, *The Power of a Man*
and *The Man Whisperer*

"Oh, mama! Doug Fields is the master of embarrassingly profound spiritual truth. Once again, he walks us to the mirror of our spiritual journey, helps us honestly assess ourselves, and then firmly and graciously points us to the possible in God. Fresh Start is my kind of book: powerful and simple. Jesus said, "Blessed are those who hunger and thirst for righteousness." Realize this blessing! Dive into *Fresh Start*."

KENNY LUCK
Random House Author of the God's Man Series
Founder, Every Man Ministries

"I'm grateful that this book is not just on *becoming* a Christian but on allowing God to help us *be* the Christians we've *become*! Life change will happen if the ideas within *Fresh Start* are planted in the soil of an open heart. They will be for your spiritual imagination like a seed of hope, rooted in the Word; applied by the Spirit; nurtured by sound, practical counsel; and watered with great stories (and a generous sprinkling of humor!) . . . the end result could be a harvest of life as God intended us to live it!"

DR. DUFFY ROBBINS
Professor, Eastern University

"For anyone stuck in a spiritual rut, *Fresh Start* provides a biblically sound lifeline fashioned out of insightful truths that are strong enough to pull even the most spiritually discouraged and emotionally broken believer back onto the road toward growth, wellness, and maturity."

RICHARD ABANES
Best-selling author of *Religions of the Stars*

"Doug Fields is one of America's finest communicators. This book is a refreshingly insightful look at spiritual growth. Every chapter is challenging, helpful, and hopeful. Doug's special style of writing will make you laugh out loud."

JIM BURNS, PH.D.
President, HomeWord
Author, *Creating an Intimate Marriage*
and *Confident Parenting*

"I really like Doug's understanding of sanctification! Thankfully God is not done working in my life, and while I read *Fresh Start* I found myself saying, "Yep, that's me!" Not only did I feel understood, but I gained some very practical help in the way that I've come to expect from Doug's books. I highly recommend this book if you're ready to deal with some issues that may be holding you back from living God's best."

CHAP CLARK, PH.D.
Vice Provost
Professor of Youth, Family, and Culture
Fuller Theological Seminary

"Journeying to the inside of our hearts to discover what's broken is never an easy expedition, and yet Doug Fields makes it simple in his book, *Fresh Start*. Even those untalked-about issues that nobody likes to address not only made sense to me but left me hungering for more. I'm excited to get this into the hands of many of my friends who can use a Fresh Start."

WAYNE CORDEIRO
Pastor, New Hope Oahu
Author, *The Divine Mentor*

FRESH START

GOD'S INVITATION TO A GREAT LIFE

DOUG FIELDS

THOMAS NELSON
Since 1798

NASHVILLE   DALLAS   MEXICO CITY   RIO DE JANEIRO   BEIJING

Published in Nashville, Tennessee, by Thomas Nelson. Thomas Nelson is a registered trademark of Thomas Nelson, Inc.

Thomas Nelson, Inc., titles may be purchased in bulk for educational, business, fund-raising, or sales promotional use. For information, please e-mail SpecialMarkets@ThomasNelson.com.

Doug Fields is represented by the literary agency of WordServe Literary Group, Ltd. (www.wordserveliterary.com).

Unless otherwise noted, Scripture quotations are taken from HOLY BIBLE: NEW INTERNATIONAL VERSION®. © 1973, 1978, 1984 by International Bible Society. Used by permission of Zondervan Publishing House. All rights reserved.

Scripture quotations marked KJV are from The Holy Bible, King James Version (public domain).

Scripture quotations marked MSG are from *The Message* by Eugene H. Peterson. © 1993, 1994, 1995, 1996, 2000. Used by permission of NavPress Publishing Group. All rights reserved.

Scripture quotations marked NCV are from New Century Version®. © 2005 by Thomas Nelson, Inc. Used by permission. All rights reserved.

Scripture quotations marked NKJV are from THE NEW KING JAMES VERSION. © 1982 by Thomas Nelson, Inc. Used by permission. All rights reserved.

Scripture quotations marked NLT are from *Holy Bible*, New Living Translation. © 1996. Used by permission of Tyndale House Publishers, Inc., Wheaton, Illinois 60189. All rights reserved.

Scripture quotations marked TEV are from Today's English Version. © American Bible Society 1966, 1971, 1976, 1992.

Library of Congress Cataloging-in-Publication Data

Fields, Doug, 1962–
  Fresh start : God's invitation to a great life / Doug Fields.
    p. cm.
  Includes bibliographical references.
  ISBN 978-0-8499-2055-4 (hardcover)
  1. Christian life. 2. Self-actualization (Psychology)—Religious aspects—Christianity. 3. Habit breaking—Religious aspects—Christianity. I. Title.
  BV4501.3.F535 2009
  248.4—dc22   2009023460

Printed in the United States of America

09 10 11 12 13 QW 6 5 4 3 2 1

**DEDICATED TO MY PARENTS,
JIM & MARGE FIELDS**

MOM—I SURE WISH DAD COULD HAVE BEEN
AROUND TO SEE ALL THE FRESH STARTS THAT HAVE
SURROUNDED OUR FAMILY. THANKS FOR A LIFETIME
OF LOVE AND SUPPORT—YOU'RE THE BEST!

CONTENTS

AN INVITATION TO START FRESH

A story is told about a factory burning down that was owned and managed by the great inventor Thomas Edison. It happened December 9, 1914.

As the factory burned, great geysers of green flame, fueled by laboratory chemicals, shot into the air. Fire departments from eight towns rushed to the scene, but the building was all but leveled. Much of Edison's work was destroyed in the process.

Many friends and well-wishers, expecting Edison to be devastated, sent messages of condolence and support. To one he replied, "I am 67; but I am not too old to make a fresh start."[1]

Within three weeks the Edison factories were restored to some semblance of order. Soon after that they were running at two shifts. The speed of the recovery, one observer said, was almost as spectacular as the disaster.

Could it be that Edison's bold words reflect the desire of your heart—to make a fresh start? Your life's work may not have been destroyed by fire, but you're ready for a fresh start. Maybe you're tired of the way things are going and you feel like it's time for something different, better, more rewarding. Or, maybe you've experienced other areas of hurt that have set you back, and now you are frustrated, afraid, discouraged, or worried. Or perhaps you just feel trapped by harmful habits, behaviors, and attitudes that keep you from being the man or woman of God you desire to become. Whatever the case, you feel *stuck*, and a fresh start sounds attractive to you. You know God is calling you to a life more abundant than the one you're experiencing right now, but you're not sure how to start anew.

If that's your feeling, this book is for you. It doesn't matter what age you are or how long you've been a Christian; fresh starts are for everybody. Don't quit. Don't panic. And don't give up. Keep pressing on in this journey to which God has called you. The good news is that you're not alone. Feeling a little stuck is normal. The bad news is that most people give up; they settle for second best; they don't start over; they stay stuck. Please don't allow that to be you. Let's start over. I'm with you in this. Together in the pages ahead, we'll look at some of the most common and defeating issues in life, issues that keep us stuck and minimize our ability to start over. By the end of the book you will have explored many realistic and practical steps you can take to enhance the work that God wants to do in your life. Let's see what happens as you keep moving forward by faith and doing the possible while trusting God with the impossible.

I'm thrilled about the possibilities of change for you!

—Doug Fields

CHAPTER 1

UNSTUCK

Back in the 1950s, a notorious gangster named Mickey Cohen controlled the bulk of organized crime in Los Angeles. Many people have heard of his heinous deeds—but few know about his faith story.

One day, Mickey heard about a young evangelist named Billy Graham who was holding revival meetings in the LA Coliseum. Southern Californians flocked to hear the famous preacher, and Mickey was curious. He knew he was leading a miserable life and that he desperately needed help, so he made the decision to attend the crusade.

During the meeting, Mickey felt God calling him to go to the altar, along with thousands of others, to accept forgiveness for his sins. Mickey admitted that he needed the new life in Christ of which Billy spoke.

Great news—right? Well, six months later, when Billy Graham came back through Los Angeles, he met with Mickey—and discovered that nothing had changed in his life. The gangster was still running drugs and putting the squeeze on people. And beyond his outer actions, his inner world still felt miserable.

Billy warned Mickey that it wasn't possible to be a Christian gangster. But Mickey felt that he couldn't start over again. When Billy pressed him on the problem, Mickey admitted that he couldn't put down his pride, wealth, and pleasures to pursue God's ways.

In the end, Mickey Cohen never did change. Sadly, he died the notorious criminal he always had been.

Even though you may have never heard of Mickey, you may be a little like him. I know I am. Here's the shocking truth: as Christians, we *all* have a little of Mickey Cohen in us. We want God in our lives, and all the good stuff He promises, but we also want what we want—even if it's harmful to us.

In a word, we're *stuck*.

Our Mickey Cohen Tendencies

Here's my confession: although I've been a follower of Christ for many years, there are still areas in my life that feel stuck.

Do you know what I mean by "stuck"? I'm not talking about sitting in the middle seat between two large friends on a cross-country flight (I've done that!). I'm talking about being spiritually stuck—bad habits that I can't seem to get under control, nagging sins that never seem to go fully away, positive character traits I should have developed by now but that are still not apparent in my life. I desperately want to go forward and find greater maturity in my relationship with Christ, but it seems as though something is always holding me back from a fresh start.

I wouldn't say I'm tempted by the "biggies." I'm not going to run out tomorrow and rob a bank or murder someone or dress up like a woman and go out dancing in search of men. (Actually, I'm not even *slightly* tempted in *those* areas—women's shoes hurt my feet.) But even as a pastor, I always acknowledge I'm just one bad decision away from being a front-page scandal. (I'm sure you've read about some of my colleagues.) So for me, one example of me being stuck is connected more with my ugly thoughts (the ones I know I shouldn't be thinking after thirty years of following Jesus), or the thoughtless, stupid words that occasionally fly out of my mouth (I should know better!). In short, the person I want to be (*really* want to be), well, I'm just not quite there yet. I feel bogged down in some areas of my life. Can you relate? I'm guessing you can.

Whenever we feel stuck, we're in good company. Even the apostle Paul—one of the "heroes" of our faith—admitted he had recurring struggles with sin (Rom. 7:15–19) . . . and he wrote half of the New Testament. He wanted to do what was right, but he just couldn't do it. And when he tried *not* to do wrong, he often found himself doing it anyway. In fact, sometimes he even did the very things he hated most!

That's being stuck.

"Stuckness" can be a problem for us and the people we love. It can sap us of hope and make us feel like spiritual failures. It can rob us of joy. It can steal our vitality, our confidence, our contentment. Worse, the things that keep us stuck can eventually grow to destroy us. But being stuck is never part of the plan for the abundant life Jesus promised in John 10:10. God wants us to be ever moving forward so we can discover the fullness of the life He came to provide. And as people who follow Him, *we* want to go forward too. We desire all the fullness of life that God offers to us. We want a fresh start with God—today!

> *I have come that they may have life,*
> *and that they may have it more abundantly.*
> —JESUS CHRIST (JOHN 10:10 NKJV)

Do you sense that there might be things in your life holding you back from living the life God intended? If so, it's not too late for something new. The Bible is clear that we *can* pull free from the place where we are stuck, and we can start again. And God loves to provide the way forward. All of creation is about new birth, new life, new relationships with Him. God sees the *new* ahead of us and wants us to be free to get there; in other words, He wants to give us a *fresh start*!

Look at the fresh start God promised Isaiah: "I am about to do something new. See, I have already begun! Do you not see it? I will make a pathway through the wilderness. I will create rivers in the dry wasteland!" (Isaiah 43:19 NLT). That's a tremendous promise, one that I believe God continues to offer today.

But maybe you're throwing up a caution flag already. You're thinking to yourself, *Wait a minute, pal! You just admitted that you sometimes feel stuck too. You're in the same bog as me! How can you possibly offer any hope and answers? Why should I listen to you? How can your book help me?*

Great questions. There are plenty of books out there already—but many are by authors who try to convince us we're *not* stuck. They say we are strong, clever, capable, and fully able to solve our own problems by determination and grit with some added enthusiasm. Their messages emphatically state, "What you believe, you can achieve!" The implication is that if we can only summon up enough inner power, or slice and dice our personalities with the right spiritual techniques, then we will inevitably buff up our lives so we can be the perfect people we need to be. God will be so happy with us—hey, *we* will be happy with us—if only we will try harder.

Surprise. I'm here with the opposite message. We are poor, pathetic, spiritually penniless sinners. We are stuck people indeed. What's more, *we* can never scrub ourselves up enough to be perfect. Our ability to start again doesn't come from our own strength or resolve or positive thinking. Neither does the power to change come from our "inner light," some kind of Jesus-consciousness or transcendental glow sticks. The bottom line is that change comes only because we can do all things through Christ who gives us strength (Phil. 4:13). We are free to change, yes, but not by our own *limited* power. Real, lasting change comes from God's *unlimited* power. Anything else is a temporary fix.

That's why I can write this message. We are all in this together. Yes, I do have times when I am stuck—just like you. I *know* I'm a candidate in need of God's transforming power. But I also know how to tune in to God so that I can access His promised power and experience change that will last. And that's what I want to share with you in this book.

Here's the good news: God knows that it's easy for us to become stuck. He's well aware of the fact that we are all honorary members of the "Stuck Club"—and yet He loves us anyway and longs to transform us. God is in the transformation business. He takes real, flawed, messy people and invites us to start fresh and live lives of fullness and forward motion. And best of all, fresh starts are available more than once. Sometimes we get *un*stuck, only to get stuck again sometime later. That's okay. God doesn't demand that we walk a tightrope of perfection. His grace is offered continually and is always within reach. God's plan is something we can all look at and say, "Yeah, I could do that."

So are you ready to grab hold of a fresh start for your life? Let's go!

But wait . . . we need to deal with Mickey Cohen first. As I said, there's a little Mickey in all of us.

The Lure of the "Stuck Club"

Let me paint a picture for you. Week after week, you go to church, desperately in need of a fresh start for your spirit. But you feel as though you're on a treadmill; you keep going and going . . . but you're not getting anywhere. You're a follower of Jesus—you know you are—and yet you feel dry and parched, desperate for God's presence. So today, you arrive at church, hoping for an exhilarating worship experience or a message from God just for you, some external influence that will trigger a spiritual fresh start. But nothing happens. And you leave just like you came.

What's the problem? Why can't you change? Why can't I change?

Sometimes it's just a bad day at church, but other times the deeper issue is that we flat out *like* being in the Stuck Club. Whatever our sin, there's something attractive about it that makes us want to hang on to it. In other words, we're just like Mickey.

But what does the Bible have to say about those sins to which we so tenaciously cling? Second Corinthians 7:1 says,

> Let us purify ourselves from everything that contaminates body and spirit, perfecting holiness out of reverence for God.

Read the verse one more time and see if you can identify the key word in the passage. What do you think it is? Go ahead and look; I'll be waiting. I think it's *everything*. Have you ever made a list of the "everything" in your life, those areas of messiness that contaminate your character and rob you of the fullness of life? Take a moment to identify just one area. Maybe it's pride, gluttony, lust, overspending, rage, worrying, cross-dressing (wait, that's twice in one chapter), guilt, depression, conflict—you name it. Do you really want to be unstuck from this area? Before you answer too quickly . . . think about it. I'll do the same. *Hmm . . .*

» Wouldn't we actually miss that feeling of power that comes from controlling other people's lives? Oh, we *say* we don't want to be controlling, but it feels pretty good once in a while . . .

» Aren't we at least a little fond of that adrenaline rush that accompanies our raging fits of explosive anger?

» Do we *really* want to be free of our lust and the exciting sexual fantasies that come with it?

There's something comfortable about being stuck. It's like wearing an old pair of jeans that "fit just right" and you don't want to get rid of them even though they're old, messy, out of style, and stained. You put them on out of habit and do so without realizing it. Same with being stuck—sometimes it just feels good. Yet stuck is draining us, sucking us down. Or at the very least, it's keeping us from a fresh start. One of the crazy things about us is that the very bog in which we get stuck—full of nasty sludge that's destroying our lives—is actually incredibly difficult to leave behind. In fact, we often don't want to!

Our questions and reservations about change seem sincere, but could it be that they are simply excuses in disguise? Have you ever found yourself saying anything like the following?

» "I know I'm supposed to read the Bible and pray, but I'm just so *busy* now—I don't have time to be the Christian I want to be. What am I supposed to do?"

» "I'd love to teach a Sunday school class, but if anyone ever found out what I do sometimes, they'd never let me teach again. How can I stop this sin?"

» "I know I should be a more loving parent, but have you ever spent time with my kids?! Whoa, baby, what they need is a strong kick in the pants! How can I ever quit yelling at them?"

» "I really should be kinder to my husband, but this is just the way I am. He just needs to realize this is who he married—I am what I am. Or can there be a better way to handle this marriage?"

» "I feel so miserable today. I know that God loves me, but I just feel like a big mistake all the time. I can't get it right, and I feel so guilty about it. Is this truly the abundant life God promised?"

So what's the answer? How do we find a fresh start when we don't know how to change—or, if we're honest, don't even *want* to change?

The key to a fresh start begins with something you may never have thought of before. It's called *sanctification*. That's a big theological concept, but don't let it scare you, because it can become a great friend when you understand it. To put it into a relatable picture, sanctification is about as straightforward as taking a nap.

How We Catch Our Z's

Think about sleep. If you've ever been around kids, you know that when they reach a certain age, they tend to resist it.

Parents say, "Go to sleep."

Kids answer back, "But I'm not sleepy."

Actually, the kids have got something there. Sleep is one of those ethereal, uncontrollable things in life. None of us can go to sleep by pure determination alone. We can't just *decide* to sleep and then sleep. Like, "Okay . . . I'm sleeping now." Click. *Zzzzzzz.*

The key is *cooperation.* I always assured my kids that even though they didn't feel sleepy, if they would just cooperate and do certain things to open themselves up to sleep, soon enough, they'd sleep.

So what did I encourage my children to do? I'd have them lie down on a soft mattress, turn out the lights, and close their eyes; and then I'd force them to listen to one of my sermons . . . and, sure enough, sleep would come. It always happened. Night after night after night.

We can't control sleep, but we are not helpless in the process either. We *cooperate* with sleep—that is, we submit ourselves to the conditions that will take us there—so that sleep can come, changing us from grizzly bears to well-rested teddy bears. That's a picture of how sanctification works. We can't control change, but we can cooperate with God—then He can turn us from our ways to His ways. *That's* sanctification.

> **sanctification** (n): the act or state of being
> purified and freed from sin

Sanctification is always a good thing. It means that no matter how stuck we are, God always welcomes us to a fresh start with the potential of change. God loves us too much to let us stay stuck in the mud. He wants us to be the people we were always meant to be. God doesn't simply want to fine-tune our manners either—He wants to change our characters from the inside out.

What's in a Name?

Throughout the Bible, God reveals Himself by several different names. One of the names I love the most is Jehovah M'Kiddish. It means "I am the God who likes to kid around"—just "*kiddish*." Actually, it means "I am the God who sanctifies you," or, put another way, "I am the God who frees you from sin." And that's exactly what happens. The apostle Paul tells us that "those who become Christians become new persons. They are not the same anymore, for the old life is gone. A new life has begun!" (2 Cor. 5:17 NLT).

Read that last bit again . . . *The old life is gone. A new life has begun*—that's the fresh start we want! And the good news is that a fresh start is not just reserved for the moment we trust Christ with our lives; it's always available. So think of what sanctification can mean. Instead of discontent, we get joy. In place of insecurity, God gives peace. As opposed to bitterness, He offers goodness. Instead of lust, God shows us how to love. Instead of those mean streaks we once had, God plants and develops patience in our hearts. And that rage? God transforms it to gentleness . . . The list of good things goes on and on. That's the type of good God we're talking about here—Jehovah M'Kiddish, the God who sets us free and gives us a fresh start. He changes us, transforms us, because He only wants what's best for our lives.

So, back to the sleep illustration. How does a person cooperate with God in the sanctification process? Great question! Let me give two false extremes that people believe . . . and then we'll look at what the Bible teaches.

First false extreme: "God, You do all the work, while I go do whatever I want." In other words, it's God's job to transform my messed-up life. Meanwhile, I don't stand accountable. I'll just "keep on keepin' on," going about life as usual (sin and all)—waiting obediently (or not) for Him to wave His magic wand and get me "unstuck." I have some areas of my life that I don't really want to change (that I know I should); and if they are going to change, it's going to have to be all God.

That's one extreme—and it's not biblical. In Romans 6:1–2, Paul fires this question at us: "Shall we go on sinning so that grace may increase? By no means! We died to sin; how can we live in it any longer?"

Sanctification does require our involvement. Let's return to our sleep analogy. We have to *want* to go to sleep and take actions in that direction if we are to succeed consistently. We can't just stay up all night with the lights on, watching TV, walking on a treadmill, hydrating with Jolt Cola—*hoping* to fall asleep. It is the same with our lives. If we really want to change, to get out of whatever rut we are stuck in, then we have to take actions in the right direction.

Second false extreme: "I need to change, so I just need to work harder." That's nothing short of a self-improvement program, and it isn't biblical either. We can't run around for twenty miles each night, hoping we get tired, then drink a gallon of warm milk and demand sleep. Sleep doesn't work that way. It's not brought about by simple determination. Neither is life change. But that's often the route we take.

What might a Christian self-improvement program look like? When I was younger in my faith, I was in absolute awe of those who had a complete command of Scripture. If a guy could rattle off Bible verses from memory, wow, he was like Martin Luther to me! So, naturally, I maniacally wanted to commit to memory every verse of the Bible.

Now, I'm not saying Scripture memorization is wrong—in fact, I could stand to memorize more of it than I have. But it's a mistake to think that a person will change simply by *working harder*, in this case, by memorizing Scripture. Even Satan knows Scripture. I've met a lot of people who have crammed their craniums full of facts and figures and Bible stories and verses but never allowed that information to influence everyday decisions and impact everyday life. It's far too easy to think we can change solely by becoming a biblical database, attending a lot of church events, and marking up our Bibles. The real transformation comes only when we put Scripture into practice by *submitting* to God (obeying His directions) and allowing Him to transform us during our practice.

Please hear me in this area. Scripture memory, Bible knowledge, times of quietness and reflection, fellowshipping with other Christians—all of these spiritual disciplines are important. They are absolutely essential for our spiritual maturity and will help keep us from being tossed back and forth by every wind of belief (Eph. 4:14). But spiritual disciplines must always go hand in hand with a desire to submit our entire lives to the Author of the Book. That's when real sanctification can happen.

The biblical position of sanctification is that there's a "God's part" and an "our part." God takes care of the POWER part; our responsibility is the *cooperation* part. We cooperate in the process while the Holy Spirit gives us the power to change. So God's Spirit *in us* does the changing, and we do the submitting to His Spirit. (I will remind you of this idea often so you'll have a firm grasp of it by the time you finish this book.)

What might that look like in daily life? Let's put some flesh on this idea.

Start with God's power. Do you know it? Do you truly believe it exists? Jeremiah 32:17 gives a glimpse of it: "Sovereign LORD, you have made the heavens and the earth by your great power and outstretched arm. Nothing is too hard for you."

I love that last phrase—*nothing is too hard for you*. Theologians call this the *omnipotence* of God. It means that God is almighty. He has unlimited power. He never gets tired. He is never frustrated. Everything He does, He does easily. Nothing is ever too hard—or even minutely difficult. It's easy for Him to answer a prayer. It's just as easy for Him to create a universe. He's all-powerful. And how do we get God's power in our lives? We ask for it; then we start to act in accordance—in other words, cooperate— with the changes we know God wants to make in our lives.

For example, let's say an over-the-top workaholic—who never has time for his wife, kids . . . or God—wants a fresh start in his battle over busyness and putting work before everything in his life. As the clock ticks toward 5:30 p.m., he's still working. But he's also busy praying, "God, give me the power to overcome workaholism. Please help me. I'm ready. I'm asking for Your help to break this self-destructive pattern in my life."

But when the clock strikes 5:30, God is not going to supernaturally pick this man up off his office chair and transport him home in time for family dinner. The man himself must cooperate. His muscles will need to move in accordance with the changes God wants to make in his life. God invites him to act in a way that corresponds to his prayers for change. But the man needs to submit to God's transforming power for himself. It's God's power that's doing the transforming—God will gladly change the man's character and desire—but the man must do his part: turn off his computer, close his office door, and drive home from work. He needs to do the possible and leave the impossible to God.

Another example: A woman, who feels stuck in a pattern of fit-throwing rage, is committed to asking God to remove this pattern from her life. She prays, "Oh, God, unless You remove this ingrained anger, I'll never conquer it by my own strength."

Soon enough, a perfect opportunity for a raging spree presents itself. The woman is at home, and her son doesn't come when he's called for dinner. Involuntarily, she tightens up to prepare for another violent outburst. But wait. She remembers that *she* must make her muscles cooperate with the changes she has asked God to make in her life. She unclenches her fists, loosens her jaw, and climbs down from the chair where she's reaching for the frying pan. She knows she can relax because God is removing rage from her life—as she cooperates by making her muscles move in accordance with the direction she's praying.

I realize life is more complex than the way I've presented it in these examples, and in time, we'll look at some of the deeper ditches that get us stuck on our way toward a changed life. But that's a fresh start in a nutshell. It's *God's power* working in conjunction with *our cooperation*.

It's when we turn out the lights, lie down on a soft mattress, and close our eyes. We cooperate with the process, and sure enough, sleep comes. It always happens. Night after night after night. And change will always happen too—God *will* transform our lives and do the impossible—when we cooperate by doing the possible.

I don't know exactly where you want a fresh start. You might be thinking specifically of your relationships, a lapsed work ethic, bad habits, or slowing spiritual growth. You want to be closer to Him, and you're ready to battle some of the issues that keep you stuck. That's great. God is ready, and this book will help you with some challenges to do your part while you rely on God to do His part.

Over the course of this book, we're going to look at some specific areas of life that derail most of us and keep us stuck. (Some of these will be surprising, because they don't even feel like disobedience.) Then we'll look at practical solutions for cooperating with God in the starting-fresh process. As we do, we will talk more about what it means to be sanctified and answer the question, what does sanctification look like in real life?

But in the meantime, in the space below, I invite you to write down a key word that describes a vision for your own fresh start; it can be anything: a person's name, a word describing what you want your relationship with God to look like, a habit you need to break, a character quality you want refined—anything. Where do you need a fresh start? What could that look like? Write that word in the blank below.

I need a fresh start with _____.

Now, how might you move forward from being stuck in that area?

Regularly, I hear people point to their messy behaviors and identify the behaviors themselves as the problem. But misbehavior is almost always a symptom of something else, looming underneath the surface—*pain*. You can find it at the root of just about any situation in which someone appears to be hopelessly stuck. It's seldom porn or gambling or overspending or eating or drinking too much that is the real issue. Instead, it's that we're in pain, and we're using these other devices in false attempts to feel better. Perhaps we're grieving or lonely or empty or annoyed or sad or angry. Maybe we feel abandoned, or a goal of ours has been blocked, or we have expectations of somebody or something, and those expectations aren't being met. Our wheels are spinning dizzily as we try to hide the real issue, but we only get deeper and deeper in the muck.

Unfortunately, if we never get honest about our pain, we will never experience a truly fresh start. Instead, we'll be ever searching for something to ease the pain—a pursuit, maybe, or a habit. Then, when we see that our choices are getting the best of us, we reach for a cover-up, a facade, *anything* we can hide behind. A mask we put on can feel like a new start—an improved-marriage mask, a better-behaved-kids mask, a life-is-fine-once-again mask, a switch-to-a-better-church mask, an everything's-okay-I'm-great mask—but really it's just a disguise to cover the pain.

What about you? It's time to make this personal again. What's your pain? Why do you *really* want a fresh start in the area you wrote down in the blank? Take some time to think through these questions:

» What's broken within you that's making life painful?
» What mask do you put on to hide your pain?
» What consequences are you reaping from wearing this mask?

Now fill in the blank that follows:

The primary pain that continually makes me stuck is: _____.

God doesn't send pain, but He does have His reasons for allowing it. Whenever you're ready, He's waiting to help with your fresh start . . . if you want His help.

Now, you and I know plenty of people who are not motivated by

God. Rather, they're pursuing a self-help kind of "fresh start." They're in pain, tired, lonely, overweight, relationally damaged, lazy, and/or financially strapped, and they understand intellectually that something needs to change. Enter the snake-oil salesman. In times of pain, it's always easy to follow some dude with big teeth who gets us fired up about walking on coals. Especially when he tells us we can discover the "power within" a whole lot quicker for three easy payments of $99.95 and an ongoing subscription to his newsletter that gives tips for blistered feet. (Am I the only one who thinks this is weird? Is the power really within *me*? Yeah? So, it's *my* power . . . but he wants to charge *me* for *my* power. Seems I should at least get a discount on my own power.)

But whenever we make life-altering changes without God at the core of our reason for change, those changes won't last. It's not a bonafide fresh start. We may think we're unstuck, but we still have one leg deeply planted in the mud.

An honest-to-goodness fresh start happens because of God. He gives us the power to change. We change for His glory. God isn't simply *one* of our many motivations to change; He is the *core* reason. It all comes back to Him.

It's *because* of God that I don't want to waste my life.

It's *because* of God that I know I need to change.

It's *because* of God that I can change.

It's *because* of God that I want to change.

It's *because* of God that I will change.

It's *because* of God that I can't settle for a mediocre and powerless life.

Look at the sentences above and decide which one applies best to your feelings about your life. Then fill in the blank below:

It's because of God that I _____.

When we make God our focus, when we hold the mirror to our hearts in the light of God's glory and holiness, we know we are in dire need of change—and quick! We evaluate the condition of our hearts, compare that to God's goodness, and we recognize the truth about ourselves. We see wicked intentions. Impure motives are magnified. And we can't do a thing about it—not alone. The good news is that seeing the truth about our hearts draws us nearer to God—nearer to His holiness. We can move forward when we say, "God, on my own, I'm a mess. But with You, I've got a shot at a fresh start."

Even when our regrets create shame, anger, embarrassment, grief, and resentment, we can still be washed clean. Psalm 32:5 says, "Finally, I confessed all my sins to you and stopped trying to hide [them]. . . . And you forgave me! All my guilt is gone" (NLT).

If you've opened up as the Psalmist did, you have the right to release the past—because God has released you from it. You're not stuck there.

The prophet Isaiah knew what it was like to be suddenly *unstuck*. How did he react to his freedom? "Then I heard the voice of the Lord saying, 'Whom shall I send? And who will go . . . ?' And I said, 'Here I am. Send me!'" (6:8). That's the "yes" of a fresh start. Isaiah had had a change of heart, and God gave him a fresh start. He was never the same again. The proof is in the rest of the book that bears his name.

And that's how it will be for you and me. Say yes to God. Let your confession sound like this:

» "I *will* do Your will."
» "I *will* do Your work."
» "I *will* live a life that honors You."
» "I *will* be the parent I need to be."
» "I *will* be the spouse I need to be."
» "I *will* be the friend I need to be."
» "I *will* be all that You want me to be."
» "Give me a fresh start *today*."

And watch what God will do with you.

CHAPTER 2

PRIDE VS. GOD-SIZED DREAMS

When I was young, I couldn't wait to grow up so I could do something great. I had some glorious dreams! What I really wanted to be was Batman. He had all the cool gadgets—like the Batmobile, Batboat, Batplane, and Batsuit—and he just looked so much cooler than most superheroes. Remember the visual sound effects from his fight scenes? *Kapow! Wham!* He could take the Joker to the mat any day.

As I got a little older, I moved from superheroes to super-career-heroes. I wanted to be a policeman or a fireman or a ballet dancer (just kidding about that one!). I could easily picture myself chasing down the bank robbers or crashing through the doors of a burning building to rescue those trapped inside.

Then for the longest time I wanted to be a professional athlete. I wasn't even sure what sport I'd play for money—all I knew was that I would be the best at it. I envisioned myself breaking tackles for the winning touchdown, swishing in the last-minute jump shot for the NBA championship, hitting a hole-in-one at the PGA Master's Tournament, zooming past the checkered flag at the Daytona 500, or catching a fish that would outweigh a Buick. (Wait, never mind. Fishing isn't a real sport . . . it ranks even below bowling.)

Somewhere along the way, the athletic dream faded. I discovered that to be a professional athlete, you actually had to be good at something. Oh yeah, you had to *practice* too—a word not even in my vocabulary as a kid.

But the dream of being someone great and doing something significant never left me. I wanted to be somebody important. I wanted to do something cool. I think most of us have similar dreams for our lives. We all dream of greatness when we are children. I've yet to meet a child who says, "I plan to strive for mediocrity . . . with the hope of achieving very little." No, as kids, we set lofty goals based on even loftier dreams.

So, as an adult now, have *you* achieved those dreams that you once had?

It's okay to say you haven't. I haven't achieved all my dreams, that's for sure. In fact, my dreams have changed so much from when I was a child, they don't even resemble the dreams I had back then. I'm not even sure you could call them "my" dreams at all. But more on that later . . .

Very few people achieve all they ever hoped to. Somewhere along the way, our dreams of greatness and glory have a head-on collision with reality. Life gets in the way: responsibility, loss, pain, paying too many dues, rejections, disappointments, relationships that require work (or don't work at all), unreasonable and unmet expectations, regrettables—it all takes its toll.

As adults it can be easy to end up doing things we never wanted to do, being people we never thought we'd be, settling for lives that are far from what we dreamed of when we were young. In the quest for our dreams, we become, as I said in chapter 1, *stuck*.

The Problem with Dreams

Why is it so easy to get stuck in the pursuit of our dreams? Maybe we tried for a while, but the goal was always out of reach. So we stopped trying and settled for a safer, more realistic plan. We didn't like that plan as much, but at least it was doable.

Or maybe we achieved some of the dreams we hoped for but found they weren't all they were cracked up to be. Maybe you got a big house, but then discovered it takes a long time to clean. You got that monstrous four-wheel drive, but it costs a month's salary to fill the tank. You got the promotion, but it's hurting your marriage. You got the cute baby, but she's colicky and keeps you up for nights on end—which doesn't help the marriage either. You got married to the perfect man, but he eats like a gorilla and you can't stand the sight.

In hindsight, have you ever been happy that God didn't allow you to reach one of your dreams? Maybe you really wanted to marry a particular person, but it didn't work out. It hurt at the time, but now, years later, you're thankful that God closed the door on that dream.

Or maybe you really wanted to have a certain career, but never got there. And you realize now the true costs that career would entail. Having God say no to that dream actually feels like a huge relief now.

One of the biggest problems with so many of our dreams is that, down deep, they are fueled by a slippery little character flaw that seems to affect the whole human race—and gets us stuck in an unbreakable cycle. It's pride. We want what we want for our glory. We want to be great. We want to be rich. We want to be significant. We want others to be proud of us or impressed with us. We want lots of stuff. We want the perfect relationship that meets all our needs. We want the wonderful family, in which nothing ever goes wrong. When we pull back the layers and honestly examine the motives of our hearts, so many of our dreams are crafted to bring about our success, our adulation, our ease and comfort, resulting in a false sense of security. The bottom line is that our dreams revolve around *us*. That's pride talking.

Does that surprise you? It wouldn't shock me if it did. I know very few people who would readily admit to having a problem with pride. Ask me to list the areas of life with which I struggle most, and I wouldn't immediately put pride at the top of the list. When I envision prideful people, I think of rock stars—or cult leaders—just add red robes and a fleet of Rolls-Royces. That's certainly not me. Is it?

C. S. Lewis once wrote:

> There is one vice of which no man in the world is free; which every one in the world loathes when he sees it in someone else; and of which hardly any people, except Christians, ever imagine that they are guilty themselves. . . . The essential vice, the utmost evil, is Pride. Unchastity, anger, greed, drunkenness, and all that, are mere fleabites in comparison: it was through Pride that the devil became the devil; Pride leads to every other vice: it is the complete anti-God state of mind. . . . As long as you are proud you cannot know God. A proud man is always looking down on things and people; and, of course, as long as you are looking down, you cannot see something that is above you.[1]

Lewis calls pride "the utmost evil." That's a bold statement. It means that pride has a sneaking tendency to drive everything—even our dreams. That's why many of our dreams fizzle and fall flat. They're built on nothing more than hot air or our own desire to be inflated.

What does pride look like? Pride is when we think more highly of ourselves than we ought. Or when we start believing we're the ones ultimately responsible for our success. Pride is a foundational sin—the one sin at the bottom of so much trouble. When it's driving our dreams, it can push us into a whole host of problems, including friction with friends and family members, workaholism, burnout, church conflicts, financial trouble, strife with neighbors, quarrels with our children's teachers, clashes at work, even trouble with the law.

Think about the various ways pride can crop up as we pursue our dreams:

Pride can take the form of *entitlement*.

We shoot for the sky but think we don't need to buckle down and work for things. Or we assume that because we've worked for things, a certain type of success is guaranteed. We deserve stuff! It's ours! When success doesn't come, we blame others, or the system.

Pride can take the form of *overconfidence*.

We work hard for our dreams in our own strength. Boldness, courage, and daring get pushed too far and become grandiosity. We whisper things like: "I really am a big shot around here," or, "I'm going to achieve my dream all on my own," or, "No one around here can do things as well as I can," or, "Everything always depends on me."

Pride can take the attitude of *superiority*.

We've come quite far in our dreams, so we look down our noses at other people and their possessions, knowledge, or behaviors. We think to ourselves: *There's no way I'd hang around with her*, or, *I'd never succumb to that sin*, or, *How did he get himself in such a mess anyhow—why can't he just pull himself up by his bootstraps?*

Pride can even show up in the form of *false humility*. Maybe we had dreams once, but we quit the race. Ask some people if they have a problem with pride and they'll say, "Not me; I'm such a loser," or, "Pride's not my problem because everything I touch turns to garbage." Feeling like a consistent loser is another form of self-focus, which is the essence of pride. And sometimes the worst arrogance of all is to declare that pride isn't an issue.

Pride can sneak up in the strangest of places. Take a look under the surface of whatever situations you're stuck in right now. Do any of the following statements sound like something you've said?

» "I hate my job. I can't believe I'm stuck in this position. Why was Jane promoted when I wasn't?"

» "I can't believe my friend lives in such a big home. Why does she get so great a house when I don't? I deserve better."

» "I should have married someone else. My spouse is okay, but I know there were better ones out there."

» "I know I stepped in line ahead of someone, but there's no way I'm going to apologize. That's just the way it is."

» "I'm so good at wielding the checkbook. Because of *my* smarts, my family's finances are sitting pretty."

» "My daughter's soccer coach is such an idiot. I could do a way better job than her."

» "My Bible study leader is so insensitive. I need to go set him straight."

» "That cop had no right to pull me over. Why doesn't he go catch a real criminal?"

» "They want *me* to help out at Vacation Bible School? I'm not going to sacrifice my vacation for a bunch of other people's kids."

» "I know I've got some bad habits. But this is just me. This is the way I am. I don't have to change for anyone."

» "Me be honest with someone? That's not the way it's done around here. We keep our thoughts to ourselves."

It can be a tough realization when we recognize pride in ourselves and our dreams. We don't normally categorize ourselves as prideful people. But when we look a little harder, pride shows up everywhere.

Let's do a little work right now. Take a few moments and think about a few of your dreams that have not come to pass. Pull back the layers of your heart and try to examine honestly the motivation behind those dreams to help determine why you might be stuck. Do any of your dreams revolve around . . .

» the desire to win at all costs?

» the need to be noticed?

» the determination to show others that you can succeed?

» the longing to be accepted?

» the need to be seen as right?

» the aspiration to be respected?

» the need to be first?

» the hope of making a name for yourself, your family, or your legacy?

» the longing to get people to value you?

» the ambitions of material comfort, wealth, luxury, and ease?

Write a few words below that help you remember your dream and the motivation behind it.

_____

_____

Can you see a subtle underlay of pride in that dream? It's okay to say yes. Many of my dreams fall into the prideful category too.

So what's the solution? How do we move from stuck to a fresh start in this area?

The answer may involve something you've never thought of before. It sounds scary at first, but it's really much gentler than it first appears: it's *elective surgery*.

And the surgeon is God.

God's Heart-Scalpel

What would happen if you laid aside your dreams, the ones that have never come to pass, the ones that got stuck in the mud? Perhaps you haven't reached them because you were aiming for the wrong dreams all along. Maybe there's something else in store for you—a new dream. One you don't have to chase after. But how do you find it?

A lot of Christians are familiar with Ephesians 2:8–9, the frequently quoted passage about being saved by grace and not works. But many of us aren't as familiar with the verse that directly follows. Verse 10 says, "For we are God's workmanship, created in Christ Jesus to do good works, which God prepared in advance for us to do."

That verse is so important. It gives us a glimpse into God's dreams for our lives. His dreams may be something we have never imagined before, yet they are far better than anything we could have come up with on our own.

You see, God created us to share in His glory. He designed us with greatness in mind—greatness in character, service, action, courage, compassion, and love—and His dreams for our lives are huge and powerful.

God doesn't want us to be stuck in pride-fueled dreams that lead nowhere near His path of greatness for us. He invites us on the journey to the destiny He's "prepared" for us. And if you'll take a look at verse 10 again, you will see that He has prepared these good things *in advance* for us to do and be. God's dreams aren't the elusive and illusory kind of pipe dreams that we have to chase after. When we draw close to Him, He works through us to bring these dreams about. But please understand: God's dreams for us are never rooted in our own self-importance; they are always rooted in *His* glory. He wants us to be representatives of *His* majesty. We become all we were meant to be as a reflection of *His* greatness. But for that to happen, our dreams must correspond to His God-sized dreams for us.

So how does elective surgery fit into that?

Part of sanctification, the process of moving from who we are, to who God wants us to become, involves a spiritual scalpel. God invites us to trade our old, broken-down dreams for His new and good ones. To do this, God asks to be allowed to cut away the questionable character qualities that have seeped into our lives. He never demands that we choose His dreams. His way is always an invitation.

But here's where things start to sound tricky. Brace yourself. The method God uses to bring these new dreams about is . . . uh . . . I hate to say it, but . . . circumcision.

Say what?!

Now, I realize that when I throw out a word like *circumcision*, some will read and gulp and begin to sweat. Others are saying, "Check, please! I need to leave quickly." But before you become hypercritical, I want you to understand that the idea of circumcision is not just a physical concept; it's also a spiritual one. And it's not just for men. It's for all. There are dozens of biblical references to it.

In Genesis 17:12, yes, God told Abraham to "circumcise" all the *males* in his household and all his male descendants. This was to be the mark of an agreement: the family of Abraham would forever be God's people, and He would always be their God. I've often wondered about Abraham's initial response. If it had been me, I would have said, "Seriously? Are You kidding me, God? How come Noah got a pretty *rainbow* as a covenant symbol? That doesn't seem fair."

But Abraham responded as he always did, in obedience, and millions of Jewish males were circumcised to show that they were God's people. This circumcision was a *physical* cutting of skin—for men only—and it was their ID card. How they showed it, and how often, I'm not exactly sure. And I don't want to know. But according to the Bible, that's how it was. It differentiated them from the Gentile nations who did not belong to God.

But a couple thousand years later, the apostle Paul wrote of a different type of circumcision. Colossians 2:11 reads, "When you came to Christ, you were 'circumcised,' but not by a physical procedure. [It was] a spiritual circumcision—the cutting away of your sinful nature" (NLT). In other passages, found in both Old and New Testaments (see, for example, Deuteronomy 10 and Romans 2), this is called the "circumcision of the heart"—and this spiritual procedure is precisely what God uses to move us—men, women, boys, and girls—from stuck to starting over.

Listen carefully: if you will allow the sin in your heart—arrogance, anger, apathy, whatever—to be "cut away," your life will look tremendously different. Through God's surgery, you will be molded into the image of Christ. God cuts out your sin . . . and puts in Jesus. With my life, I've experienced less Doug, more Jesus. Less pride and self, more humility and service. Less worry, more peace. Less anger, apathy, and angst; more love, compassion, and contentment. Less junk, more effectiveness. Less heartache, more joy. It's not an easy surgery, but it's a good one.

Then—and only then—are you free to do all of those "good works, which God prepared in advance for [you] to do" (Eph. 2:10), *without* the trappings that keep you stuck in an immobile and fruitless state. That's *God's* dream—for me and for you.

New Dreams Ahead

Let's review: When it comes to moving from stuck to starting over, the big picture is that God wants us to resemble Him. He wants us to be Christlike. He accomplishes this via this crazy thing called "spiritual circumcision"—removing what's unneeded from our hearts so that our character resembles His. So how does this actually happen? Does God just take a big spiritual knife out of the sky and slash away?

Remember, the biblical arrangement for sanctification, or purification, includes a "God's part" and an "our part." God handles the POWER part; we are responsible for the *cooperation* part. While the Holy Spirit is inside us, doing the changing by His power, He invites us to cooperate with His Spirit within. The real work is always done by Jesus. He transforms us supernaturally by performing the heart's "circumcision." Our part is to stay close to Him through the Word and by prayer. As we get to know Him and yield our lives to Him (or, as I said in chapter 1, act in accordance with the changes God wants to make), He does the real work of changing us. But never forget, it all hinges on *our* cooperation.

What might this cooperation look like? How can we even begin to voluntarily (let alone enthusiastically) replace our pride-fueled dreams with God's great dreams for us? Let me suggest one foundational act of compliance that will help tremendously in this area. It's what I call "taking a knee." Apart from its use in football, *taking a knee* is my own personal phrase to help me remember the concept of humility.

To most of us, humility feels like a posture of submission, and few of us like to be submissive to anything. You might even think humility is synonymous with being wimpy or weak—and no one wants that. After all, followers of Christ are supposed to be victorious—right? Certainly, we think, Billy Graham never "took a knee." After all, he was the spiritual advisor to presidents, prime ministers, kings, and queens. Beth Moore doesn't take a knee, does she? She speaks to millions of women all over the country. Rick Warren can't possibly take a knee—he prays at presidential inaugurations, writes best-selling books, tells me what to do, and occasionally yells, "Booyah!"

Let me just say that I know personally only one of the people I just mentioned, so I can't speak for all of them, but I can say without a doubt that, as victorious as Rick Warren is, he takes a knee often. And my guess is that's also true for the others. Humility is an incredible sign of spiritual strength.

Think about it this way: when a warrior comes back from battle and sees his king, he takes a knee, not out of weakness but out of an understanding of who the king is. He takes a knee to show that he willingly submits to a higher authority.

Humility isn't a position of weakness; it's a position of power. Humility acknowledges by an act of will that God is God. But there's something ugly inside us that wants to keep us off our knees and keeps humility at a distance. That something often comes alive when we think someone else might be winning, or getting what we want or deserve. You know what that "something" is called? It's the same thing that fuels empty dreams. Yes, it's pride. Again and again . . . pride lives.

Taking a knee is the opposite of pride. It's an act of humility, and it allows someone else to be the star. Humility says, "I can let you have your way; it's not a big deal to me. God is my audience. I don't need to compete with you." A humble person doesn't have to prove himself with words or actions. A humble life speaks for itself. That's not weakness. It's the very picture of strength.

The best example of humility was Christ Himself. Philippians 2:6 says that "though [Jesus] was God, he did not demand and cling to his rights as God" (NLT). And get this: Paul prefaced that verse with this admonition: "Your attitude should be the same that Christ Jesus had" (v. 5 NLT).

Yet, if I were to make a list of one hundred ways that Doug Fields is not like Jesus, tops on the list would be how it could never have been said about me that I "did not cling to my rights as God." If I were the God-man, I'd let everyone know about it. I'd have a God badge. A God bumper sticker. I'd have a billboard in my yard—GOD LIVES HERE! I'd have God Night at Angels' Stadium. And I'd have a movie about me called *Doug Almighty*. Oh yeah I would!

But Jesus took a knee: "He made himself nothing; he took the humble position of a slave and appeared in human form. And in human form he obediently humbled himself even further by dying a criminal's death on a cross" (vv. 7–8 NLT). This was Christ's life: Born *humbly* in a manger . . . He *served* others . . . He was *obedient* to God the Father . . . and He *submitted* Himself to the worst punishment man could dish out: torture—and a brutal death.

None of those are acts of weakness. All of them required undeniable strength. Jesus was a strong, humble man. And His humility was honored in the end: "Because of this, God raised him up to the heights of heaven and gave him a name that is above every other name, so that at the name of Jesus every knee will bow, in heaven and on earth and under the earth, and every tongue will confess that Jesus Christ is Lord, to the glory of God the Father" (vv. 9–11 NLT).

That's an example of a God-sized dream—and it starts with humility.

Now, God doesn't promise that people will bow at our feet if we are humble. But we *will* be honored. That's a promise: "Humble yourselves under the mighty power of God," begins 1 Peter 5:6, "and in his good time he will honor you" (NLT). And further, "humility brings honor" (Prov. 29:23 NLT). We don't know exactly what *honor* will look like in our lives, but we do know that "with humility comes wisdom" (Prov. 11:2 NLT).

Wisdom and honor—those are incredible rewards. I want those rewards in my life—how about you?

Let's put this into practical terms. What could humility look like for you? Let's look at some examples of taking a knee and being rewarded:

» Instead of retaliating, you reconcile.
» Rather than always doing the talking, you actively listen.
» You say, "I'm sorry"—even when it's very difficult.
» You choose discomfort so others can be comfortable.
» You take a personal loss so someone else can win.
» You serve even when you haven't been asked—because you see a need.
» You make others feel good about themselves.
» You take the spotlight off yourself and shine it on others, making *them* the heroes.
» You refuse to be cocky, no matter what your qualifications (or level of insecurity).

Instead, you journey through life with a confidence in *God*.

Humility is what God wants most for you. And if you will commit to developing it in your life by cooperating with God and walking in His direction, He will bring to fruition *God-sized dreams*.

A Fresh Start for Your Dreams

Are you ready for a fresh start in relation to your dreams? It's never too late. But you'll need to be prepared to exchange your old, worn-out dreams for God's new, unlimited one. Your original dreams, like mine, were probably born of pride, anyway, as we discussed in this chapter. God asks for your willingness to allow Him to perform a spiritual circumcision to cut away that pride and to shape you into His image. But it's by invitation; He won't strong-arm you into cooperation. Instead, He *invites* you to cooperate with Him, to "take a knee" and trade pride for humility.

Are you ready for this? If so, get ready for a fresh start—and some God-sized dreams.

CHAPTER 3

THE STRANGE INGREDIENT OF SUCCESS

I recently went to a high school basketball game and had a great time! Two top local teams battled it out, basket for basket. I love going to high school basketball games, because everything's so pure. It's just the smell of a freshly varnished gym floor, the pounding in the bleachers, the silly chants from the teenage audience, and the joy of watching unpaid competition. The game is completely unadulterated by the glitz of professional sports—like when I played in the NBA . . . *ahem.*

But I must say that in spite of all the fun, something disappointing happened that night during the pregame ceremony. It was Senior Night, and all graduating athletes were introduced along with their parents. An announcer highlighted some of the players' basketball accomplishments, then read what each boy had written about his plans for the future. And one after another, each teenager's goals began to sound the same:

"Jason plans to attend college, with the hope of landing a great job that brings in lots of cash."

"Chris will attend university this fall with a goal of becoming a millionaire by the time he's forty."

"Gabe will go to MNO College and wants to be financially secure."

"Brandon wants to be a successful entrepreneur with lots of money."

"Michael dreams of a bright future with lots of wealth and two Ferraris."

It wasn't just a few of the boys who spoke of such materialistic goals; it was the majority of them.

I sat there thinking, *Adolescence meets the American dream: free enterprise defines success in a high school gym.* One boy even described his life's goal using the title of rapper 50 Cent's super-hyped album *Get Rich or Die Tryin'.*

Really? Where do eighteen-year-olds get these types of goals? Is this what we are passing down from generation to generation? "Son, to really make your life count—bigger is better. Loot wins! True greatness means having a lot of cash." Although sad, the words of those young people echoed through the gym long after the pregame ceremony was over. In their minds, success was synonymous with making it rich. At such a young age, it seems like they *already* need a fresh start.

What emerges in adolescence has a way of chasing us into adulthood. Our bodies change, but often our values remain the same. Think about it as it relates to your life. What's your definition of success? Might you have something equally trite that you're chasing as intently as these teenagers are? Or is your definition of success a little broader than being financially secure? Success, to adults, usually means being in committed loving relationships, receiving respect from our children, living in peace, possessing integrity, having self-respect, staying healthy, and developing strong, united, caring networks of family and friends.

None of that is wrong. It's just an incomplete definition of success. It's missing the core ingredient of true success, the type that remains successful even if everything else in that list fades away. We'll talk more about what true success is in the rest of this chapter.

The problem comes when we examine our lives and ask ourselves if we've achieved true success. The answer is often no. We may not have reached our goals, or if we have, perhaps a strange sort of emptiness has ensued. In the wake of our achievement, our onetime definition of success has left us cold. We may not be able to articulate what real success is now, but we wish we knew what it was. Our old pursuit of it feels as empty as a gymnasium after a basketball game.

The Problem with Chasing Success

Sometimes, just like those eighteen-year-old basketball players, even we adults still seem to closely link our definitions of success with material wealth. Money drives our dreams. It's a key motivating factor in how we set goals. It's a foundational principle behind decisions we make.

But at other times, we are chasing something else. Maybe it's meaning. We chase it because we don't want to waste our lives. We may not care about material success, but we definitely care about significance.

Or perhaps we're chasing security. We're content with little and don't really care to make a great name for ourselves. Above all else, we just want stability and predictability. Success by this definition means never having the boat rocked.

Whatever our definitions of success are, there's something pumping in our guts that says, "There could be more!" And, actually, this is right. There *could* be more. And according to the Bible, there *is* more. I'm betting that you'd like to know God's take on true success. It's very different from the world's definition. The biblical definition of success . . . is Christlikeness.

When Jesus walked the earth, He taught that significance, security, and material wealth aren't all they are cracked up to be. He promoted a different kind of success and a different way to get there. He said that real success, authentic greatness, is to become like Him. What does that mean? Let's look at His own words: "Whoever wants to become great among you must be your servant, and whoever wants to be first must be your slave—just as the Son of Man did not come to be served, but to serve" (Matt. 20:26–28). In short form, "If you want to be truly success-ful . . . you've got to serve."

Serve? Really?

Is anyone besides me a little disappointed by that radical recipe for success? If I were God, I would have picked something different. But for God, it's very clear: the route to greatness is paved with service.

Here's what the Bible shows us: Jesus served. Meeting the needs of others was His lifestyle. He healed, listened, helped out, stopped to talk, and put others' agendas before His own.

Once, Jesus' closest followers were fighting over which one of them was the greatest. The story is recorded in Mark 9:33–35. Jesus and His disciples were traveling, and along the way, the disciples argued among themselves. Their brilliant conversation went something like this:

"*I'm* the greatest."

"No, *I* am."

"Uh-uh. How can you be the greatest when, clearly, *I'm* the greatest? You're just stupid."

"I'm not stupid. *You're* stupid."

"I know you are, but what am I? You're the stupidest person I know."

"Am not."

"Am too—er—*are* too."

Then Jesus sat them down and redefined greatness. He said, "If you want greatness, if you want true success, I've got a very different road for you to travel. It's different from what the world tells you. If you want success, you must *serve*." The NIV puts it this way: "If anyone wants to be first, he must be the very last, and the servant of all."

Jesus' formula for greatness dropped jaws back then . . . and it still does today. We want greatness, but we don't want *that* kind of greatness. When I think of greatness, I immediately think of Muhammad Ali. In my era, he had a famous motto for which he was known. He'd always say, "I am the greatest!" He meant it too. I'm not sure he was familiar with Jesus' "the servant of all" teachings!

I once heard a story about a flight attendant telling Ali that he had to buckle his seat belt. (I'm not sure if it's true . . . but it sounds right.)

"No, I don't have to," Ali answered, "because I'm the greatest."

"I'm sorry," said the flight attendant, "but it's the rule. Everybody has to buckle their seat belt."

"I'm an exception to the rules," Ali said. "Superman don't *need* no seat belt."

With a smile, the woman replied, "Superman don't need no airplane."

The moral of the story? Even the self-proclaimed greats have to occasionally face reality.

Biblical reality is that a successful life isn't based on narcissistic principles. It's based on selfless ones, and a selfless person—like Christ—serves.

I'd like to think that if Jesus were the coach of that high school basketball team, He would have called the players to Him after the pregame celebration and said, "Boys, I love your ambition. That's what makes you such great young men. I truly care about you and want what's best for you, and because of that I want you to know that chasing the dollar isn't going to give you what you're ultimately looking for. If you want to be great—*really* great—then you've got to learn to make serving others a natural part of your daily life." After all, even He came "not to be served but to serve others, and to give [His] life as a ransom for many" [Mark 10:45 NLT]. And who was greater than Him? No one was ever more significant!

One of Jesus' best examples of service happened just before the cross, when He pulled His disciples together for a final meal. He knew His hour had come to leave the world and return to the Father. But before He left them, He wanted to show His disciples the full breadth of His love. "So he got up from the table, took off his robe, wrapped a towel around his waist, and poured water into a basin. Then he began to wash the disciples' feet and to wipe them with the towel he had around him." When He had finished, He said, "[Now,] I have given you an example to follow. Do as I have done to you" (John 13:4–5, 15 NLT).

Let's camp here for a minute. Foot washing was not an unusual action in early Judeo-Roman culture. But for a teacher such as Jesus to do so—a respected rabbi—it was highly unusual. Normal for a servant, yes—but not for a man of standing.

So why did Jesus choose to wash His disciples' feet? Why not their hands? Feet are nasty. Even in our present age of perfumes and powders and Odor-Eaters . . . feet stink. Imagine back then, when people walked everywhere on dusty roads. People's sandaled feet encountered camel droppings and mud puddles—no street sweepers and no homeowners' associations keeping things clean. People had dirty feet. Really dirty feet. Think, *dreadlocks for the toes*. And that fact wasn't lost on the disciples. So when Jesus got up to clean their feet, it was a total shock. Why didn't Jesus choose some other act of service? He could have opened a door for them, or pulled out their chairs. But those options were too effortless, too ordinary, too easy.

One of my best friends has the stinkiest feet on the planet. He loves to needle me too, so whenever we're in a meeting or restaurant, he takes off his shoes and counts how long it takes before I notice and say something (yeah, real mature, right?). The thought of washing his feet literally nauseates me. I'd rather have a pack of jackals attack my neck than wash his feet.

Yet the last life-lesson Jesus wanted to give His closest friends was for them to see Him serving by washing their feet. They had heard Him teach about service. Now He wanted to drive the point home by show-ing them an example, as if to say, "Boys, *this* is success; this is greatness. It's the opposite of what you think. It's not about pride; it's not about making a great name for yourself. It's about service—*it's about washing feet*. Now . . . go and do likewise."

Jesus drove this truth even deeper when He served not just the Twelve but all of humanity by going to the cross so others could live. For Jesus, serving wasn't just a nice idea—it was the main idea. The utmost act of service was giving His life for others. But since giving our lives *for* others (through death) will probably never be part of the package for you and me, giving our lives *to* others—through service—is precisely the path God has chosen for those who want genuine success.

Why is it so tough to serve others?

Sometimes it's because we think we're too busy. Or we don't quite know what to do. Or we wonder if our acts of service will be well received.

But usually, service is tough because of one primary thing: we're selfish.

That's true for me. I'll admit it. I'm majorly selfish. Not mildly selfish, mind you, but grossly selfish. I'm running for president of my own fan club, and I'm not dropping out of the race. I like me. I like me a lot. I like you too, but not nearly as much as I like making sure my needs are met.

How am I selfish? I have enough examples to fill bookcases. Here's one recent example: Last week I had an easy opportunity to serve my wife, but I totally blew it. I got a wild idea and decided to clean out our closet. One of my brilliant decisions was that I wasn't going to hang up my T-shirts anymore because they made the closet crowded. Only one problem: what do I do with all my "can't-get-rid-of" T-shirts now?

I knew that my wife had extra room in her armoire—if only I cleaned it for her. Now, the armoire has three shelves, and all three were pretty disastrous. So what did selfless Doug do? I cleaned off one shelf, put my T-shirts on it, and left the other two shelves messy. My reasoning: they were *her* shelves. It would have taken me a grand total of ten minutes to clean and organize her other two shelves, but I didn't. I was so proud that all of my T-shirts fit in *her* dresser. I'm telling you—it looked so good!

Unfortunately, Cathy wasn't quite as impressed as I was. It was *her* armoire, after all. Let's just say, my whole plan didn't go over too well. And my insensitivity stood out as plain as the T-shirts that are currently and conveniently resting in a storage bin under our bed. (We'll leave it at that—we're still addressing the situation in counseling.) Bottom line: I had an opportunity to serve my best friend—in such a small, easy way—and I didn't. That inaction turned into a big deal.

How about you? In what ways are you selfish? Let's do a little self-test. As you know, the battle is always between what comes naturally and what we know is spiritual (following Jesus' example to serve). When you see something that needs to be done, what's your first tendency?

A person's natural tendency says something like this:

- » "I don't want to."
- » "Why me?"
- » "Someone else can do it."
- » "I'm very busy."
- » "I don't *feel* like it."

A person's spiritual tendency says something different:

- » "I can do that."
- » "Let me help you."
- » "Let me put aside my agenda and come alongside you."
- » "It's an honor to serve."
- » "I don't feel like it, but I'll do it anyway."

Which tendency is most prevalent in your life? I'm convinced that once someone admits his or her own selfish tendencies, that person is well on his or her way to becoming unstuck on the journey to true success. (Ever heard the saying "Admitting is the first step to reform"?) Only when you become aware of your natural resistance to serve others, can you begin to see clearly God's plan for greatness.

Meaningful, effective service is seldom easy. But if we want a fresh start in our spiritual walks, we must serve. Serving is the primary method God uses to form the character of Jesus in us. When we serve, our lives are being morphed into the likeness of our Lord. We are never more like Jesus than when we serve. Service is the main ingredient in the recipe for greatness and success. It's also the antidote for emptiness.

God wants you to embody service. He wants it to flow naturally out of your life. Even to define you. So He invites you to serve, not out of obligation but out of desire.

Cooperating with God

I fulfilled a lifelong goal recently when I ran the San Diego marathon. It sounds more impressive than it was—actually, it was more like me wheezing through it. (Running indicates speed, which I don't possess.) The race organizers had hundreds of volunteers to serve the thousands of runners, and after the race, I struck up a conversation with one of the volunteers. Okay, I'll admit it . . . he was giving me oxygen. Anyway, I asked him why he was serving at the event.

"I feel so much better when I serve," he said. "Why do you ask?"

"Well, I'm doing some informal research about serving for a book project," I said. "It doesn't surprise me that you feel good when you serve. I'm convinced that the reason why you feel different is because God created you to serve. He draws people nearer to Him when they do."

The volunteer swallowed and looked at me like I was an escaped psycho and he was giving me too much oxygen. I may have frightened him a little more when I asked him to continue serving and give me a piggyback ride over to my car. He ran away instead.

Let's recap the logic flow so far:

We pursue our definitions of success, but the type of success we pursue often leaves us feeling empty. Our definition embraces what we want in life: love, meaningful relationships, security, peace, purpose, wealth, contentment . . . and the Cubs finally winning a World Series. These are basic wants, and they're not wrong. They're just incomplete.

The incompleteness shows up when we don't get these things. We feel stuck. We want to move from stuck to starting over, but we don't know what to do. How do we get a fresh start?

Culture says, "Chase, consume, conquer, and rule your domain."

But Jesus says, "You've got it all wrong—serve others."

A fresh start is activated when we choose to move from *selfishness* to *service*. And when we do, we are living a new definition of success: Christlikeness. This success is fulfilling. It doesn't leave us feeling empty or stuck or defeated, because it is the model of Christ Himself, and He is neither stuck nor defeated.

Okay, let's make this practical. How does this transformation actually happen? How can we move from service as an obligation to service as a regular part of our lifestyle?

The real work is always done by God. I've said that all along. He transforms us supernaturally. But we must make the *choice* to cooperate with Him. If we really want to change—and be a servant by choice rather than a servant by resentful compulsion—then we must ask for His help, stay close to Him, and then yield to Him by voluntarily moving in the same direction we're praying.

Let me suggest some practical acts you might consider.

Eliminate Excuses

An opportunity for service presents itself, and your first tendency is to weasel out of it. Normal? Yes! I know this one well . . . I am King Weasel.

But you know that God wants serving to be part of your character.

So what can you do to cooperate with that expectation? Begin by deliberately eliminating your excuses.

What's your favorite excuse? What tends to keep you from jumping at acts of service? Take a minute to write down your default excuse in the space below.

What keeps me from serving is usually _____.

Did you write, "Too busy" or "Time"? Survey says . . . [*ding*] . . . those are the top answers.

I believe that many of us are genuinely busy people. We live active, full lives, and there are several legitimate activities and interests that grab for our attention.

Still, there's an old adage that says, "You always find time to do the things you want to do." Proof?

A while back I was talking to a high school student at my church. He had just received an iPod for Christmas, and he was boasting of the thirteen thousand songs he had loaded on it. I asked him how long it took to download all those songs onto his iPod. After he gulped a few times and scratched an imaginary rash, he said about two hundred hours.

Something stirred in me. My response wasn't characteristic of my normal, gentle, pastorly self. "Two hundred hours!" I exclaimed. "You've got to be kidding! Too bad you didn't spend some of those same two hundred hours serving others. God would have taken those serving experiences and not only blessed you on earth with a sense of significance but also rewarded you in eternity."

He had the same look as the marathon volunteer and probably wanted to run away. But instead, this teenager looked at me with big tears in his eyes. "Thank you for being so wise, Pastor and Jedi Master Doug," he said. "You're completely right—as you always are."

Actually, what he really said was, "Dude, you sound like my dad," and walked away. But I hope he got the point.

I hope you do too. Many times we make serving excuses that have become manufactured by misplaced priorities and poor decision making. It's amazing what happens to our time when we make something a priority.

Start Small

One of the amazing things about serving is that God can take something that is a seemingly small act of service and turn it into something very big. If you haven't noticed, God has a long history of promoting the "small factor."

> » Jesus took a small amount of bread and fish offered by a small boy and made it big enough to feed thousands (John 6:1–14).
> » Jesus used the widow's offering of two *small* coins to illustrate for all time how big her heart was because she gave her all (Mark 12:38–44).
> » Jesus said that even a cup of water (definitely a *small* thing), given in kindness, is big enough to reap a great reward (Matt. 10:42).

So, when you begin your lifestyle of serving . . . my suggestion is to start small.

Some people have a tough time starting small because they have bought into the cultural myth that "bigger is better." (You know what I'm talking about—"go big or go home"?) I see this type of thinking at my church all the time. We have more than twenty thousand people attending weekly, and the size of our church can really keep people on the sidelines. They think, *This church is so big; the buildings are so big; the video screens are so big; the pastor is so . . . nice. If I'm going to serve, it better be big.*

But personally, some of my favorite acts of service at my church are the "small" things, the ones many people probably don't know exist. Guys show up on Saturday mornings and serve by mowing the lawns.

Others serve by cleaning the restrooms in between services. They serve by stuffing our bulletins, sharpening pencils, picking up trash, cleaning out communion trays, washing my car between services. (Yeah, I wish. I'm hoping someone from my church will read this book.)

When you're serving, God looks at your heart and rewards your *motive*, not the size of the job—He cares about your heart's condition (1 Chron. 28:9).

Start small. See a need and meet it. That's the simplest equation for serving and success. Service, with the right motive, is never small to God.

Serve Together

One of the favorite parts of my life is getting to serve with others. Some of my best friendships have developed as a result of serving together. I often thank God because I don't have to do ministry alone. I think that's maybe how Jesus intended for it to happen. Just look at Mark 6:7—Christ called His twelve disciples together and sent them out two by two. The early church was built on Christians serving together.

What happens when you serve together? Two people working as one get more done than two people working independently on the same goal. The project multiplies and mushrooms, and pretty soon it grows to where you're feeding tens of thousands of homeless people in your neighborhood. That happened at my church recently. Some people got their heads together and met with some other folks who had the same vision, and soon enough, more than forty thousand homeless people in Orange County were fed. I guarantee that if all the hundreds of volunteers who were eventually involved in that effort had tried to work on the problem by themselves, the result would not have been nearly as successful. We were better together.

When you serve together, you find more fulfillment and joy. The highs are intensified, and the lows don't sting nearly as much when they are shared.

Keep Looking

If you think your ideal place of service is working with children, but then you discover that you actually hate snot and runny noses . . . keep looking for other opportunities.

If you want to help out with teenagers at your church, but then realize you want to date them . . . uh . . . definitely keep looking.

You may try serving somewhere and then feel it wasn't a good match for you . . . *keep looking*. For example, maybe you think you're a really good teacher and believe you have the gift of teaching. You put yourself in a position to teach, then realize that while you may have the gift of teaching, others apparently don't have the gift of listening.

Don't give up on serving! Keep looking for other opportunities.

God has wired you to find deep fulfillment in serving Him. Tragically, only a fraction of the Christian population ever experience the thrill of serving God, because they don't get into the game and keep looking until they discover their giftedness.

Sometimes, a place of service looks different than you ever imagined it would. It may not be your ideal place, but you see a need and respond to it. For instance, I know of a former NFL player who finds great joy in serving at his church. He was a starter, a high-achieving all-star, and his tackles made opposing players' organs switch positions. As a follower of Christ, he has decided to serve by emptying the trash at his church. The guy is worth millions—he could afford to pay for the entire janitorial service with his pocket change. Instead, the guy empties trash. I've heard he also works in the nursery (the little ones' size reminds him of a football). This man has learned the value of service, and he has intentionally decided to incorporate it into his life—even if it means starting with the trash.

Regularly Rest and Reflect

When it comes to service opportunities, there is always something more to do. Opportunities never end, because people always have needs.

But there's a danger here—of trying to meet all the people's needs all of the time. That's why, every now and then, we need to take a break, rest, and reflect.

Even Jesus took breaks. He set boundaries for His life. He knew when to say no, when to walk away, when to take time for Himself in places of solitude and restoration.

A life of continual service is what we are called to. Still, continuous service can feel overwhelming at times. There have been times throughout my years as a pastor when I've driven by that McDonald's down the street, seen the Help Wanted sign, and thought, *Hmm, that might be a nice place to work.* I could simply clock in at 9 a.m., work the ketchup gun until 5 p.m., then clock out and go home. When I'm home, no one would call me with emergency hamburger problems. No one would complain that the sundae I served them wasn't meeting their needs. No one would tell me that something I said while working behind the counter rubbed them the wrong way, that they hate me, and that they're thinking of leaving McDonald's forever and attending a different franchise down the street.

Here's reality . . . service is work, and sometimes it can be *really* hard because people are involved. At times you are misunderstood, ignored, or slighted. People want help, but they want it a certain way, and you can't deliver, or at least they say you can't. There are times when all your efforts don't do *anything* to help a situation. And occasionally, serving can be downright painful. It brought Christ to the cross.

Let's return briefly to Mark 6. When Jesus sent out His followers in pairs, they returned all fired up from serving. Many leaders today would seize that opportunity to work their volunteers even harder. Jesus Himself could have pushed for more achievement—both in His disciples' lives and for His plan. But notice what He did instead. He said, "Let's get away from the crowds for a while and rest" (v. 31 NLT). And they left by boat for a quieter place.

Did you catch the significance of that? Needy people were all around them. More service opportunities. Unmet needs. There was plenty more to be done. But Jesus took His disciples out of the action for a while, even though they had just experienced an extremely positive time of serving. Why? Because He knew His disciples needed rest. Burnout wasn't part of His plan. He wanted them in the game for the long haul. And part of His strategy was encouraging His disciples to build regular times of solitude and relaxation into their lives.

That's such an incredible lesson for us today. Serving should never be at the expense of our personal spiritual health and development. It should grow our faith, not choke it out.

A Fresh Start Toward Success

Okay, so has "success" eluded you thus far? Do you want a fresh start? Do you want to lead a *truly* successful life? If you've paid attention to this chapter, then you know that the key ingredient isn't more money, a better relationship, a more glamorous job, or having more friends. According to Jesus, the key to a successful life is service. And in a nutshell, service is nothing more or less than seeing needs and responding to them. It's rolling up your sleeves and getting the job done in Jesus' name.

Does that sound like a strange pathway to success to you? It's okay if it does. It's the opposite of what the world tells us to do. The pop-culture way is to chase and conquer, climb and claw.

But Christ says . . . *serve.*

When you serve, you experience life as Christ experienced it. He came to serve others, and when you do the same, you experience more of Christ in your life. That's success, *authentic* success. And it's the route to your fresh start today.

:: CHAPTER 4

BEYOND
YOUR PAST

Wouldn't it be nice if the results of all our wrong choices in life were painless? Imagine if, whenever we made bad decisions, we could simply pull over, swing a U-turn, and move on. No real loss ensues. No significant pain results. Our poor choices amount to no harm, no foul, no consequences. Mistakes are no problem. Sin is no big deal. Just move on.

It's nice to fantasize about, but unfortunately, that's not reality.

So many times in life we come to a crossroads where we have an opportunity to choose God's way or the world's way—and we make the wrong choice. Now, I'm *not* talking about life's no-brainer questions, like these:

» Do I attend small group or commit arson?

» Do I tithe or rob a bank?

» If I rob the bank, does God still want a 10 percent tithe?

Most of our daily decisions aren't this black and white. Most of them involve more complex circumstances, like these:

» *How we use our money*—do we manage it God's way, or conduct our financial affairs according to the world's values? Say, for example, my accountant made a mistake on last year's taxes. To fix it will cost me an extra five thousand dollars that I don't have. Nobody will ever know about the mistake if I keep silent. So what do I do?

» *How we think about sex and sexuality*—whose value system do we embrace? The one we see in advertising, in magazines, and on TV—or God's design that is spelled out in the Bible? *God wants me to be happy, right? And that means having a fulfilling sex life, right? And currently I'm not happy, so God wants me to do something about it, right? So that means leaving my spouse and looking elsewhere for fulfillment—right? If not geographically, at least in my mind . . . Right?*

» *How we respond to friends and family*—do we treat one another based on God's standards, or do we depend on the relationship advice of our favorite radio or TV hosts?

» *How we view work ethics*—God doesn't want you to be unfulfilled, but you're not fulfilled at your current job. Maybe you even *hate* it . . . so that gives you license to slack off, right? Or at least daydream at your desk and spend excess time on your fantasy football team. Doesn't it?

While many of us say we choose God's way, the truth is that the world's mode is often easier to follow. Our mainstream culture can be attractive, alluring, even seductive—tempting us with its ease and its reward. I know many people who want to identify with God, but in moral and ethical realms, they take the easiest way possible—the one that mirrors society at large. They embody a situational integrity based on convenience. And that's not integrity at all.

Jesus warned us that traveling God's way would be difficult. "Small is the gate and narrow the road that leads to life," He said, "and only a few find it" (Matt. 7:14). Now notice what He said about the world's direction: "Wide is the gate and broad is the road that leads to destruction, and many enter through it" (v. 13). Jesus was saying that the way of the world is easy to travel—but it also leads to harm. We are free to choose, but we are not free from the severe consequences of going down the wrong road. My hunch is that many reading these words have stories and scars from that type of travel.

How about you? Do you have a tale of woe (and the battle scars to prove it) about a wrong road you have taken? I'm sure you have, and you're definitely not alone. But to quote the great theologian Pumbaa, from *The Lion King*, "You gotta put your behind in your past."[1] That's a key step toward a fresh start.

I desperately want to know God's way and walk in it. And I want to make my decisions with clarity, confidence, and conviction. I want that for you too, and so does God. But sometimes guilt over previous wrong decisions can really keep us stuck. In fact, one of the biggest obstacles to moving forward is guilt from our past. We've all made wrong choices that carried great cost. Perhaps we're still paying the price for them. Now, on top of that, we also have to deal with the guilt of those decisions. *Guilty, guilty, guilty*, the little voice in our head says. *And who do you think you are, trying to move ahead after all you've done?* Let me help you: that voice is not your friend. You know who it really is—and you need to tune him out. The enemy wants you to stay stagnant, stuck in the quagmire of remorse. But God wants to give you a *fresh start*.

Our Suburban Sins

I must confess—I don't have a wild and raunchy past that would make for a best-selling action movie. Actually, I don't even have the type of past that would make for a good episode of *Sesame Street*. My history is fairly bland—not very colorful at all—pretty much beige with a few scattered streaks of tan. Thankfully, I became a follower of Jesus as a teenager, and I haven't had too many worldly experiences that resulted in extreme emotional, spiritual, and relational disarray. I admit it. I'm unable to relate to a lot of worldly actions:

1. I've never worked the red-light district.
2. I've never bred illegal prizefighting cockatoos in my carport.
3. I've really never inhaled.
4. I've never committed Enron-style white-collar crime.
5. I've never spent time in a biker gang or hanging with homies in my crib.

In fact, growing up, my crib was actually a crib, and "pimping my ride" meant I was getting new handlebars for my bicycle.

For some, that might be enough reason to stop reading. I hope you don't. But I acknowledge that you might be thinking, *Well, then, how can you even relate to my past? My life . . . well, let's just say that my past makes you look like a monk.*

Don't get me wrong—I occasionally express a worldly "wild side." Sometimes I'll empty my shopping cart without returning it to its parking lot cage. And when I'm in my "mean mood" there are times I don't recycle. While I may not have the sordid résumé of some, I know God clearly sees my very real sins.

Once, when I was sixteen, I was supposed to go to McDonald's and pick up food for the whole family. Coming home, I couldn't stop myself with the fries. I ate them all. I knew my family would be bummed that there were no fries, so I lied. I acted surprised. I told them the kid behind the counter must have forgotten to put the fries in the bag. *Little white lie.* But it's not about the size of the sin; it's about the sin. Even if that had been my only mistake (and it wasn't), sin separated me from a perfect and holy God. Little sin, big sin. Sin leaves a residue of guilt . . . regardless of size.

So it's obvious that I'm not Charles Manson Jr. . . . but, let's be honest, most people who choose to read a book like this aren't either. Often, our sins are neither huge nor obvious. We're not running from the law. We're not hiding criminal records. We've never spent time in jail. We just do boring-sin stuff, and do it over and over and over.

But we're still haunted by our pasts. And our present-day lives are checkered with memories of our poor decisions—things like:

» sexual sins we're not proud of;
» financial blunders we're embarrassed to admit;
» people we have hurt;
» relationships that went sour because we blew it;
» shameful actions spurred by anger that got out of hand;
» substance abuse and a subsequent criminal record;
» recurring bad habits we just can't seem to shake;
» jobs we lost because we took what wasn't ours; or
» shameless displays of pride, lust, envy, rage, or hatred.

For all these things and more, we suffer guilt. And that guilt is a roadblock to pursuing your best life now.

Do you have a past that is less than stellar? Can you identify with feelings of guilt, shame, regret? If guilt is now holding you back, spiritually or otherwise, you may be saying things to yourself like this:

» "Why would God want anything to do with me?"
» "Who do I think I am that God would use me?"

» "How can I teach people to live God's way, when I can't even consistently do it myself?"

» "What if people knew the *real* me, with all my flaws and blemishes?"

That's the language of someone who's dying for a fresh start.

It's not only Christians who fall into this trap. I have a non-Christian buddy with whom I've been friends for years. I've invited him to church so many times that I've actually wanted to stop inviting because it's starting to feel obnoxious. He's a great guy! He's not anti-God, but he's clearly not a follower of Jesus. This week I invited him again—and he rejected my invitation again. His reason? "My past wouldn't play well at church," he said.

That's being stuck. It can be easy to feel that way. But what if I had said to him, "Hey—no problem, bring on your past. We'll make a movie of it and show it on the big screens. We have huge screens at church. I'm sure your past *would* play great!"

What if I said that to *you*? What if I had some kind of machine that could capture your past and project your all-time worst moments on the screen? How well would your past play?

Actually, when you and I relive our pasts, nothing very good usually comes from it. Guilt quickly follows, and it's a thief. Here are some different kinds of guilt and the negative effects they can have on you if you don't put your behind in your past—er, that is, your past behind you—and embrace a fresh start:

Guilt That Separates from Salvation

An example of someone being robbed by this kind of guilt is my buddy. He's not a bad person, but neither is he someone you could call a Christian or Christ-follower. His guilt is separating him from the free gift of salvation.

Like my friend's past, your personal history may be keeping you from becoming a follower of Jesus. You may be thinking, *Yeah, I can relate. I'm interested in spiritual matters, but my past wouldn't play well with God, and I'm definitely not good enough for Him.*

Guilt That Separates from Service

This kind of guilt stymies the person who has a relationship with God, but whose past is keeping her from being used by God. If this is you, then you probably look at others doing things for God and wish you could be used, but you can't imagine *yourself* being an instrument in God's hands. You can't see how your scarred life can be used to do anything good for God. You're just thankful for the seat in heaven with your name on it—meanwhile, your past is keeping you on the sidelines.

Guilt That Separates from Intimacy

This guilt relationally incapacitates its victim. The person is definitely a Christ-follower and is even serving in a ministry somewhere. But he finds it difficult developing intimacy with God because of the past he remembers and replays in his head.

If this describes you, you're trying to walk God's way—you really are—but your past is like a stain on a treadmill belt—you just keep seeing it over and over. It bothers you, and you believe it bothers God too. You know God has forgiven you, but you still think He's disappointed in you. And you're certain that the closer you get to Him, the more clearly He will see that stain. Your guilt is robbing you of a warm, intimate relationship with the God who loves you.

To help you move beyond your past, I want to show you someone in the Bible who did exactly that by *cooperating* with God (refer back to our discussion of sanctification in chapter 1). This man had a treacherous past and yet overcame it and spent the remainder of his life traveling God's way. His name is Saul, and his past will make you look like an Eagle Scout with an untucked shirt.

Saul's Story

Saul's story unfolds in three parts: (1) an eventful past, (2) a genuine conversion, (3) an amazing transformation.

An Eventful Past

In Acts 7 we find Saul standing at the death scene of Stephen, a strong follower of Jesus. Here's the context: Jesus had been crucified, He had proved He was the Messiah by rising from the dead, and He'd now ascended to heaven. Those who saw Jesus after His resurrection had moved from "maybe He's God" (the way they thought before the resurrection) to "He's God and I want everyone to know it" (after the resurrection). They understood that if Jesus didn't rise from the dead, He'd be just another famous dead guy.

Stephen had experienced Jesus after the resurrection and couldn't keep quiet about Him. Because of that, he was stoned to death. People literally picked up rocks and hurled them at his head until he died.

What was Saul's role?

As Stephen was being dragged out of the city and people began to bash his head in with rocks, the rock throwers took off their coats and laid them at the feet of a young man named Saul. Saul was one of the official witnesses at the killing of Stephen.

This image is very powerful! You can almost see Saul standing next to the bloody scene. It's a stand of approval. A posture of power. On his face is probably a look of disgust toward a follower of Jesus who would allow himself to be killed for what he believed.

The Bible says that after Stephen was stoned, a great wave of persecution began that same day. It swept over the church in Jerusalem, and all the believers except the apostles fled into Judea and Samaria.

What a scene! Persecution hits, and instead of driving the followers of Jesus away from their mission to tell others, it actually scatters them out so that the message spreads and increases. They may have feared for their lives, but the fear sent them on new roads that resulted in the message of the good news getting out all around. But it wasn't all good . . . back to Saul. As if his one act of holding the coats for the stoners wasn't enough, Saul was fueled into a horrible action. He began to lead the charge in persecuting Christians: "Saul was going everywhere to devastate the church. He went from house to house, dragging out both men and women to throw them into jail. . . . Saul was uttering threats with every breath. He was eager to destroy the Lord's followers" (Acts 8:3; 9:1 NLT).

Saul became a key ringleader in the anti-Jesus movement. Unlike today, when those who are anti-Jesus have limited power—a microphone, a Web site, a TV show—Saul wasn't limited; he had the power to destroy. His goal was to devastate the early church. By his own admission, later in his life, this is what Saul said about himself: "I caused many of the believers in Jerusalem to be sent to prison. And I cast my vote against them when they were condemned to death. Many times I had them whipped in the synagogues to try to get them to curse Christ. I was so violently opposed to them that I even hounded them in distant cities of foreign lands" (Acts 26:10–11 NLT).

Okay, so it doesn't take much intelligence to know that Saul's past was—well—despicable. He was a man with innocent blood on his hands. A murderer of Christians—people whose only crime was believing in Jesus as the Messiah. Saul's past was bigger than a mere character flaw.

Fortunately, Saul didn't stay rooted in his past. During his reign of terror . . . he experienced an authentic conversion—and got a fresh start.

A Genuine Conversion

Saul was heading down a pathway toward destruction, and God got ahold of his life. It was as simple as that. And it was as dramatic as that. Saul moved very suddenly from a persecutor of Christians to a passionate follower of Jesus. The Bible actually records the details of Saul's conversion in three places (Acts 9:1–19; 22:6–16; 26:12–18). One day, as Saul was heading toward Damascus to arrest and imprison more Christians, an amazingly bright light flashed all around him. He fell to the ground as the voice of God said to him, "Saul! Saul! Why do you persecute me?" (Acts 9:4). The bright light blinded Saul. But it was the beginning of his conversion.

I find it interesting that Saul tells his own story twice in the book of Acts. That's a lesson for us. One of the ways we can move beyond the past is to talk about it. It's not that we want to rehash or glory in our old sins; the aim is always to give glory to God for bringing us through those times. (We'll discuss this more in chapter 11.)

If you ever think your past is too hard to release, note that Saul's background was so eventful that his conversion was actually difficult for some to believe. Acts 9:26 says, "When Saul arrived in Jerusalem, he tried to meet with the believers, but they were all afraid of him. They thought he was only pretending to be a believer!" (NLT).

But soon Saul convinced them of the truth. God had radically changed his life and given him a fresh start. A genuine conversion can never be disguised because it will always result in an amazing transformation.

An Amazing Transformation

When I hear the word *transformation*, the image that comes to my mind is a caterpillar becoming a butterfly. The English word used to describe that process is *metamorphosis*, from the Greek verb *metamorphoo*, which means "to be transformed." When a caterpillar becomes a butterfly, it goes through a total change of being: a metamorphosis. If the butterfly imagery is too wimpy for you, think about the movie *Transformers*—big trucks totally transformed into giant robots and squashing pretty butterflies!

In Saul's life, we see an immediate metamorphosis after his conversion: (1) a destroyer becomes a follower; (2) a man on an anti-Jesus mission becomes a missionary for Jesus; (3) a terrorist becomes tender.

It was amazing and immediate. Acts 9:20–21 describes the change: "Immediately [Saul] began preaching about Jesus in the synagogues, saying, 'He is indeed the Son of God!' All who heard him were amazed. 'Isn't this the same man who persecuted Jesus' followers with such devastation in Jerusalem?'" (NLT).

That's a quick snapshot of Saul. You get the picture. The guy had a past that wasn't exactly honoring to God. But there's a lot more to Saul. He eventually got a change of name—to Paul—and he ended up writing about half of the New Testament. Paul experienced such a transformation that he even wrote, "Follow my example, as I follow the example of Christ" (1 Cor. 11:1). That's called a turnaround.

Now, let's turn this around from Saul to us.

So What Does This Mean for You?

How does the story of Saul apply to your life?

If you're not a follower of Jesus Christ—I am thrilled you're reading this. God wants to take your checkered past and guide you to a genuine conversion. A transformation occurs with God at the center of your life. A new life opens up to you. You are invited to experience the preferred life and the God-sized opportunities He has planned for you.

Just like the people who were amazed at Saul's transformation, some people are waiting to be amazed with the transformation in your life. Your past is not too bad for God. Don't miss out on a genuine conversion because of your past.

In 1 Timothy 1:15–16, Paul described his life before he met Christ: "Christ Jesus came into the world to save sinners—and I was the worst of them all. But that is why God had mercy on me, so that Christ Jesus could use me as a prime example of his great patience with even the worst sinners. Then others will realize that they, too, can believe in him and receive eternal life" (NLT).

When Paul talked about "believing in Christ," it meant believing that Jesus died to pay for our sins. Because of the work Jesus did on the cross, our pasts can disappear. Gone!

Here's an image of what God wants to do with your past. Imagine I am holding in front of you a sheet of butcher paper. Let's say this paper contains a description of the things you've done in your past of which you're not proud. Some people would have a large sheet of paper; some would only have a scrap. But regardless of the size of your past, everyone holds a sheet of paper. No one is perfect. That's the bad news.

The good news is that when we ask God for forgiveness, it's as though He comes along with a huge blowtorch and lights the paper on fire. The old is gone. Forever.

Or maybe you're already a follower of Christ, but your past has you sidelined. You intellectually understand that Jesus paid for your past with His death on the cross and that, in God's eyes, you're forgiven. But you can't imagine why God would ever want to use someone like you. What's my encouragement here?

You've got to move past your past . . . God has.

The Bible is filled with men and women with rough pasts, just like Saul, and yet God used them to make a difference in the world.

» Moses killed a man and hid his body in the sand, yet God still used him to free an entire nation.
» Abraham lied about his wife and endangered her safety, yet God still used Abraham to birth a nation.
» David committed adultery with Bathsheba. After she became pregnant with his child, David had her husband killed and quickly married her to make the pregnancy seem "legitimate." Yet God still used David in mighty ways.
» Peter denied Christ—claimed he didn't even know the man. Yet God still used Peter big-time.
» Barnabas was a hypocrite (Gal. 2:13), yet God still used him to play a vital role in the early church.

There is no sin God can't forgive. There is nothing you have done in your past that God can't redeem. The straightforward encouragement here is to know that, if you've asked God for forgiveness, He has forgiven you. Remind yourself of this every day if need be, because God wants to use you.

But perhaps you're someone who's already being used by God—maybe even in a great way—yet you feel distant from Him because your past is creating a barrier to intimacy. The closer you get to God, the more you feel exposed for what you really are.

There's a great example of a fresh-start attitude found in Romans 4:7–8: "Oh, what joy for those whose disobedience is forgiven, whose sins are put out of sight. Yes, what joy for those whose sin is no longer counted against them by the Lord" (NLT). Do you know who wrote that? Paul was quoting King David, a guy who, as I just mentioned, was an adulterer and a murderer earlier in his life. King David truly understood forgiveness—and he called it a joy.

The joy of forgiveness should draw you closer to God, not keep you distant. If God has let go of your sins, now it's your turn to let go of them—God doesn't want them standing stubbornly as a barrier to a meaningful, intimate relationship with Him. Stop reaching back into your past and pulling those sins out. Again, think of the sheet of butcher paper being burned. When you've asked God for forgiveness of your sins, your sins are but ashes.

With a Little Help from Your Friends

Sometimes it can be hard to work through feelings of guilt on our own. Intellectually, we know we're forgiven. But practically speaking, it's harder to truly feel forgiven. Our guilt still haunts us no matter what we know is true.

In times like these, a small group of trusted friends can really make the difference. Talking to other people about what you've been through can help bring about those practical feelings of "no condemnation" that the Bible teaches (Rom. 8:1). If you're feeling guilty for sins for which you've already asked God for forgiveness, these are some good steps to take with your small group:

1. Read and reflect on verses that talk about forgiveness, including 1 John 1:9; Romans 8:1; Psalm 103:12; and 2 Corinthians 5:17.
2. Pray consciously and intentionally for forgiveness of your past.
3. Talk to each other about your pasts in the spirit and attitude of James 5:16, which says, "Confess your sins to each other and pray for each other so that you may be healed. The prayer of a righteous man is powerful and effective." Allow your Christ-following friends to affirm what you know to be true. You're forgiven, truly forgiven. Your past is behind you. Hear those words. Remember those words. Feel those words. Live those words.

And say it aloud: "My past is gone. *Truly* gone! Thank You, God!"

A Fresh Start Today

No matter where you've been or what you've done, your past doesn't have to block the process of change and your steps toward God's ways. The sting of guilt and shame does not need to be a consistent part of your life. God has made it clear in His Word that even someone who has lived a darkly eventful past, such as Saul, can be converted, transformed, and used for great fruitfulness and effectiveness in Christ. That can be you!

Can you imagine what your life might look like if guilt weren't keeping you stuck? Well, it doesn't need to slow you down anymore. When you begin to walk with God, you don't need to constantly look in the rearview mirror to make sure your past doesn't catch up with you. It's gone. God's forgiveness changes *everything*. You are free for God-sized opportunities. That's the power of a fresh start.

CHAPTER 5

FREEDOM FROM HURT

There's this guy I used to work with. I'll call him Satan—I'm sorry, I mean Stan. I'll spare you the sordid details of what he eventually did, but let's just say it involved lying, stealing, manipulating, and having a sexual relationship with a girl in our church's youth group.

When all of his actions became public knowledge, I felt furious, hurt, betrayed, and devastated, because he was someone I had once highly respected. I wanted nothing to do with this guy ever again. I didn't want to see him, talk to him, or think about him. I resented how he had betrayed not only the trust of so many people—ministers, parents, and youth—but my trust as well. And I hated what he had done to that teenaged girl. I was angry at how it damaged the youth ministry. And I was completely floored when I learned he had taken his snakelike charm to another church and was trying to do the same thing there.

Have you ever felt betrayed by someone you trusted?

People are funny creatures. We need people in our lives, even though relationships can be so complicated. God wired us for relationships. When God created humanity, He said, "It's not good when you're alone." In the DNA of our genetic makeup, we long to be connected to others in a way where we are known and loved and accepted.

I recently created a survey for some informal research I'm doing on relationships. One of the questions was, "If this was your last month on earth, what would you spend time doing?" More than 7,000 people took the survey, and the number one response by far (75 percent of responders) was "Spend time with family and friends." No other answer even came close. "Get spiritual life in order" was a distant second. "Having sex" received only 420 votes (and 90 percent of those responders were single males under 21).

I'd agree with the top response. If I only had one month to live, it certainly wouldn't be spent watching reruns of *Friends* or polishing my car. It would be spent with others. Why? Because people are valuable to a healthy life. I need other people in my life—and so do you!

But relationships are messy—just like the friendship I used to have with Stan. The paradox is that we need people, but people have the amazing power to hurt us. That's hard. Chances are good that you've experienced the same type of hurt. You might even currently have pain in your relational world. Maybe it's with a friend. A spouse. Your kids. A boss or a coworker. A neighbor. Someone at church. A relative.

Whenever we experience pain in our relationships, it's easy to get sidetracked on the spiritual journey. You may want to go forward with what you know to be true, but there's this one dark area of your life. The hurt caused by another person's actions fills you with rage, depression, annoyance, or frustration. Anytime you see that other person or think about him or her, the same hurt gets replayed in your soul—and you're convinced there's just no way you can forget what happened.

Do I even need to say it? Okay: *you're stuck.*

How Do We Love Messy People?

Face it: most of the heartbreak, stress, and damage in our lives come as the result of what other people do to us. Sometimes it's what we do to ourselves, but usually it's from the messiness of others.

One consoling fact is that we are all this way—messy, I mean. Here, this will be fun: right now, turn to the person in closest proximity to you and say, "You're messy!" You might be in a coffee shop, at an airport, in a bookstore, or sitting on your couch at home. If you don't know the person, just say, "I bet you're messy."

Did you do it?

Were you punched?

Sorry if you were. But in a chapter about forgiveness, it's important for us to acknowledge that we're all in this strange relational chaos together. Every single person on the planet is, at some point, flawed or weird or even downright creepy.

I mean, *everyone*.

Including me.

And you. (Hey, you just called a complete stranger messy.)

After almost thirty years of working in the church and observing humanity, I have concluded that nobody's completely normal. Everyone is whacked-out to some degree. There are no exceptions. If you think you're the exception, you're not. You just lack the self-awareness to know that you're a crazy nut job too. We all love to think that other people are nuts while we're the poster child for normal.

Recently, while preaching at my church, I asked the congregation, "How many believe that other people are weird and you're fairly normal?" Most hands shot up.

What was the point of this little exercise in honesty?

Since all of us are a little wacky, it affects our ability to have good relationships. Relationships are painful and chaotic and hard! Right now there are 6.5 billion people running around the earth with free will, exposing their own selfish agendas, bumping into each other. It's amazing we haven't already turned the planet into a giant smoking hole in the universe.

Fortunately, God understands that we humans are relationally challenged and in need of a relational fresh start. In this chapter I want you to look at what happens when someone hurts you. What do you do? Since we've all just admitted we're faulty people, another good discussion to have would be, when we hurt someone else, what do we do then?—but we'll save that for another book. Right now, I want to challenge you to take a tough step and go back and repair some of the damage that others have done to you. Why?

Well, we could talk about how difficult it is for us to walk around with our feelings hurt all the time. And it's true; being affected by others' messiness does hurt us. But there's an even more important concept to grasp up front: Jesus calls us to love others, even if they are unpleasant and have hurt us. And if we don't love others, we can never step forward into the good plans Christ has for us.

Check out Matthew 22:36–39, where Jesus is asked, what is the most important commandment? Jesus says that loving God comes first. Loving people is second. Being right with God and being right with others is part of God's design for living life to its fullest. In fact, God's invitation to a great life can only happen in the context of a strong relationship with Him *and* with others. Both of those relationships must be clicking for you and me to live life the way God intended. They're not independent of one another.

For instance, you can't come to church and work on your relationship with God while at the same time plotting revenge and harboring anger for others. You can't sing, "I love You, Lord . . ." while eyeing someone and in the same breath whispering, " . . . but I hate her, God, and I plan to slash her tires after church." God says that's wrong on every level. So if we feel stuck in our relationships, particularly if others have hurt us, the big question to ask first is, "How do we start over and begin to love?"

Thankfully Christ teaches us how to love. Or actually, Christ transforms our lives so that we're able to love people—even hurtful people, people we need to forgive. Remember that the real work is always done by Jesus. He's the one with the POWER. As I've said over and over, He transforms us supernaturally. Our biggest invitation is to stay close to Him, getting to know Him better and asking Him to help us love those who have broken our hearts.

Yet we are also invited to cooperate with Him in our effort to love. We do this by intentionally moving in the direction we're praying.

But how on earth do we do that?

Danger: Pain Ahead

Just last weekend a guy told me about a couple who obviously had a troubled relationship. One evening, as the husband was sitting quietly, reading his newspaper, his wife walked up behind him and whacked him on the head with the back of her hand.

"What was that for?" he asked.

"That was for the piece of paper I found in your pants pocket!" she retorted. "It had the name Mary Lou written on it."

"Oh, that was from two weeks ago, when I went to the racetrack," the man said. "Mary Lou was the name of a horse I bet on."

The woman thought for a moment, then hung her head. "Oh, honey," she said quietly, "I'm so sorry. I should have known there was a good explanation."

A few days later the man was watching a ball game on TV when his wife walked up and hit him on the head again, this time with an iron skillet, which knocked him out cold. When he came to, he asked, "What was that for?"

She replied, "Your racehorse just called."

Offering forgiveness when we've been hurt is very difficult to do. Yet Jesus taught that forgiving others is vital for our spiritual well-being.

In Matthew 18:21–22 Jesus invites us to make it a priority not only to forgive but to keep forgiving, and not just seven times, but "seventy *times* seven," if that much forgiving is required (NLT, emphasis mine). The point is not the number 490. It's that Jesus wants us to be abundant in our forgiving. He wants us to forgive every day, and keep forgiving . . . all the time, if need be. What's more, those verses indicate that forgiving others is not an option or a suggestion. It's a biblical command for those who follow Christ. And we always have a choice whether or not to obey. Forgiveness is a choice to obey. Unforgiveness is also a choice—to disobey. It's seldom easy to forgive people, yet obeying God is an act of will. It doesn't matter if we feel like forgiving others or not. Obeying God cannot be based on our feelings. It's a decision we make to cooperate with God.

So why forgive? Because God said so, and He knows what's in our best interest. He knows that if I don't forgive, the following situations will typically result:

My Anger Is Intensified

Whenever I don't forgive someone, it only hurts me more. The initial hurt has already taken place. But, mistakenly, I think that holding on to my anger will in some way punish the offending party.

Nothing could be further from the truth. The offender often doesn't even realize he or she has hurt me, so I end up adding fuel to the fire that's already burning in my gut, and that's all I accomplish. My sorrow and hurt turn to resentment, and resentment always hurts me more than the other person. It's an irrational waste of energy to think my carrying a grudge will wear out the other person!

Resentment never works. Job 5:2 says, "To worry yourself to death with resentment would be a foolish, senseless thing to do" (TEV).

Think about it:

» Resentment can't change what's been done.
» Resentment can't resolve the problem.

» Resentment doesn't change the person who offended me.

» Resentment doesn't even hurt that person . . . it only hurts me.

I've never talked to anyone who has been resentful and said, "I feel so much better being resentful . . . yeah, this bitterness thing has a real calming effect on me. I feel peaceful. I'm really living." No, it's the exact opposite. The unhappiest people I know are those who carry a grudge. Not forgiving others is a slow, emotional suicide. Resentment drives bitterness into all areas of life.

I Relive Painful Experiences

If I don't forgive someone, the offense keeps coming back to haunt me, again and again.

For instance, when I was in sixth grade, a guy named Rick stole my bike. It was a good bike—not a fancy Schwinn, mind you—just a sweet, light-blue Huffy purchased at Kmart (home of the Blue Light Special). Even though Rick got caught and my bike was eventually returned, I still hated him for stealing my bike. I wasn't about to forgive him!

Years went by, and eventually I grew up a bit and managed to forgive Rick. But imagine if I hadn't forgiven him. For the rest of my life, every time I met someone named Rick, I would relive my anger. Just the name Rick would bring up the painful experience. It would be impossible to work at my church (where Rick Warren is the pastor). Maybe I would even hate bikes now too, and bicycle shops. I'd probably despise unicycles too—half as much. Stupid, huh? So is resentment.

I'm not that far off, am I? Someone once said that refusing to forgive is like drinking poison and hoping the other person dies. Unless we forgive people, it becomes a vicious cycle that eats away at us. Unresolved memories torment us. Whenever we relive pain, the other person doesn't feel a thing. He or she is out dancing and living it up, and we're at home, chained to our personal sewer, and the stench is seeping its way into our veins and circulating into our hearts.

What's interesting—and sad—is that some of us enjoy reliving the pain. It becomes the story we use to gain attention and sympathy. Whenever we rehearse the tale of being wronged, even to an audience of one, we become center stage. For a brief moment we feel important. To forgive the offending person would take away our identity—we're the hurt one—and we can't give that up. To forgive would be like taking the boat from the fisher, or the keys from the janitor, or the car from the chauffeur, or the bricks from the builder. We'd lose our franchise.

But whenever we nurse a grudge, it grows larger and stronger, like a malignant tumor inside our souls. And although we think we can hide it, in time it will take over our whole being. We'll become monsters of hostility and unhappiness. A lack of forgiveness will eventually kill us.

Or at the very least give us ulcers.

If that describes you, let me challenge you to a higher level of loving other people, even the ones who have harmed you. I know how threatening this can feel, but it's the right thing to do, and it's a response that God will honor and bless.

So how do you get unstuck from the muck that is unforgiveness? Let's walk through that together . . .

Beginning to Forgive

To be honest, I wish that I could give you a magic wand—some miraculous healing device that's guaranteed to work every time you wave it.

But, sorry, no magic wand exists. Relationships aren't that simple. Every relationship is unique, and every relational breakdown is different, layered, and complex. I have found that so-called surefire formulas are seldom worth much.

From Scripture and personal experience, I can offer a few overarching actions that will help. When you've been hurt and you want to move forward, consider putting into action the following suggestions:

Admit You're Hurt

Christians are sometimes encouraged to be false with their feelings. We're told to ignore what's inside us, to "just forget about that," or "just pray about it." But hurt tends to pop out eventually.

Or we're told to repress our hurt, to live like it never happened, to pretend it doesn't exist. But that's just denial.

Sometimes we're urged to minimize hurt, to say, "It's no big deal; it's over now. Forget about it."

But emotions are part of God's design. He created them. When someone has hurt us, it's a good thing to acknowledge that hurt. Call the truth of a situation what it is. You can't get over your hurt until you admit you were hurt. You can't even begin to consider forgiveness until you own up to what it is that hurt you. Admit it, people have hurt you.

For instance, a few years after the situation with Stan, I was in Nashville, speaking at a convention. I walked with a friend of mine to the room in which I was about to speak, and I looked up. In the very front row was the guy who had hurt me so badly. He didn't see me, but I saw him, and my stomach rose up into my throat.

My friend saw me turning pale and asked, "What's going on?" I couldn't say anything. Not there, not then. But suddenly I was faced with my own lack of forgiveness. I had buried all these emotions, but when I saw the guy again, everything came up. I knew I hadn't forgiven him. So what did I choose to do? Right then—nothing. I bumbled through the seminar with Stan sitting in the front row, smiling and living like he had actually been forgiven. Inside I was dying. And it got worse—I chose to hide.

For the rest of the week I made every effort to ignore this guy. It was a terrible week. It could have been a great time of ministry; instead it was days of misery. Since I was one of the main speakers at the convention, I had a backstage pass to nearly every event, but I was trapped by my hatred for this guy. It became very clear to me I hadn't forgiven him.

How do you admit something like that?

Thankfully, it often doesn't require some in-your-face type of confrontation. You know—get everybody together and sit the offender down and duke it out. In years since, I've found that one of the best ways to admit that I'm hurt and I need to forgive is simply to write it down on paper. That's something everyone can do.

It works like this: Get specific with who has hurt you and what that person did. Make a list of everybody who has harmed you, what they said, what they did. Put it down on paper so you can look at it. The list sheds light on denial. In front of you are the people who are keeping you from living life to its fullest. You might as well know who they are.

Who might be on the list?

- » The teacher who embarrassed you
- » The parent who said, "You'll never amount to anything"
- » A former spouse/boyfriend/girlfriend who was unfaithful to you
- » The person who never repaid the money you loaned
- » A business partner who cheated you
- » A boss who fired you

Write the name (or names) down and admit your hurt. Identify the people who did you wrong.

Determine What He/She Owes You

The next step is this: think. If you were able to sit down with the person who hurt you and have a conversation, what would you want from him or her? Write it down.

It might be something like one of these:

- » My best friend owes me an apology.
- » My boyfriend owes me an explanation.

» My boss owes me respect.

» My ex-spouse owes me a marriage.

» My ex-roommate owes me $1,500.

» My dad owes me a childhood that he robbed by working too much. He was never home to tuck me into bed.

» My mom owes me freedom from all the years she tried to control me.

» My ex said he loved me but he stole my purity. He owes me at least a show of remorse.

» That jerk owes me his life. He was the drunk driver who ran the light that took my sister.

Big or small, whatever it is, write it down. What has been taken from you? What do you think the person who hurt you owes you?

Why is this effective? When you write down what you think you're owed, you see the size of the debt. You further identify what was taken from you, and what might be done to make it right. You will probably never get that thing you want, but at least writing it down articulates your feelings. It puts things in black and white for you, and out in the open.

You may want to put your list away for a few days to make sure everyone is on it who needs to be. Every time you get mad, or have an imaginary conversation with the person who hurt you, write down what you feel is owed to you.

Once your list is complete, it sets you up to do one of your greatest acts of cooperation with the Holy Spirit.

Cancel the Debt

The third action is to write a huge PAID IN FULL over your list. Write it in red pen. Write it big. It may sound silly, but this is much more than an exercise in self-help.

To cancel a debt means that . . .

» you let go of your right to hurt the offender back;

» you let go of your desire to see the other person hurt;

» you let go of your (real or imagined) plan to get even in some way; and

» you consciously and deliberately say to the offender, "You don't owe me a thing anymore."

Here's something practical to help in this area: once you've written "PAID IN FULL" on your list, bury the note in the backyard. You might want to put a cross on top of the dirt pile as a reminder. Or burn the list. Invite a small group of trusted friends over for the bonfire, and celebrate your release. You've been stuck in hurt, pain, and anger, and it's time to celebrate and start over. Whenever you do this, you are saying to your debtors: *I have decided that, although this offense might never be put right in the way that I want, I am releasing you from the obligation I feel is owed me. In canceling this debt, I'm not going to:*

1. *hold your action against you,*
2. *raise it back up with you, or*
3. *use it against you anymore.*

Understand that simply canceling a debt doesn't settle all questions of blame and fairness. It can be easy to raise objections. To cry foul. To still say, "But they owe me!" I know! The exercise doesn't right the wrong that was done. It doesn't bring about the repentance of the offender. Your father can't return your lost childhood; an apology doesn't erase a bad experience; and an offending person can't return your job, your lifestyle, or your loss.

In so many cases, the wrong can never be made right. What was destroyed is destroyed. But it does release you from resentment. That's the power. The key is for you to release the harm that the offense keeps causing you. Cancel the debt that's owed you. Let go of resentment. Forgive the offender.

It's not easy. You may need to cancel the debt several times. I know some who have canceled a debt and they felt permanently released the first time. I know others (like myself) who needed to work through that exercise several times. But eventually you'll be free from the chains that bind you to hate, and you'll have a fresh start toward becoming the person God created you to be.

Release the Offender Completely

Whenever you write "PAID IN FULL" over your list, you consciously and deliberately say, "I release my offender. I let him [or her] go. I will stop holding on to the hurt by forgiving him." That's releasing an offender. If you don't do this, you continue to give that person power and control over your life. The offense continues its burn. You must release it as you release the offender. It's in your best interest to do so.

It's important that you understand that releasing an offender has nothing to do with waiting until the person comes to you and asks for forgiveness. That may never happen. Mrs. Finkelstein, my elementary teacher, is not going to track me down and apologize for calling me a dunce in front of the class many years ago. Chances are good that Stan will never ask for forgiveness. You release people whether they ask for forgiveness or not because you're doing it for your sake, not for theirs.

Releasing an offender doesn't mean you remove his guilt. His personal repentance is between him and God. Release also doesn't mean the reconciliation of you and the offender, because that's a two-way street. But you extend forgiveness, release him, and when and if he finally repents and confesses, you are wholly ready to reconcile with him, thus completing the forgiveness package.

Meanwhile, though, you shouldn't wait to begin the process. Resentment is hurting you and keeping you stuck. To get a fresh start, you have to forgive—now.

When It's Truly Gone

How do you know when you have fully released and forgiven an offender? Here's a short checklist:

» You can think about the offending person without it hurting sharply anymore. There may be a lingering sadness, but you're not bleeding.

» You can pray genuinely for God's blessing in this person's life.

» You can talk about the situation without speaking badly of the person.

» You can begin to look at (or think about) the person, understanding the hurt he or she has gone through, and feel compassion for that individual.

The conclusion (so far) of the "Stan" story is this: A while ago my family and I were in San Diego for a long weekend. As we walked into a restaurant, I saw Stan. He was with a woman who wasn't his wife. What he had gone through in the meantime since I knew him, I wasn't sure, but I knew it wasn't good. It was obvious he was embarrassed.

Here's the good thing: when I saw him, my anger wasn't there like when I saw him in Nashville. My stomach stayed in my stomach region. Instead, I actually felt sorry for him. I had a genuine compassion for him. This guy had a habit of messing up his life and the lives of others, and that's a very hard lifestyle to sustain. Along with my compassion, I felt a strong sense of peace. I wasn't raging inside anymore. It took me a few years, and several times of mentally forgiving this guy, but I was finally there. I needed to forgive, and keep on forgiving, and keep forgiving, until finally I could see this man and it didn't hurt anymore. I had released the offense, and it was gone. I was the one who benefited.

Maybe you're saying, "Great for you, Doug, but . . .

» . . . how do you forget a divorce?"

» . . . how do you forget being abused?"

» . . . how do you forget being abandoned?"

» . . . how do you forget being molested?"

The answer? I doubt if you ever can *forget*. Some things that happen are so horrific they tend to burn into a person's memory and reside there. Such sins are deep violations that leave painful wounds. It will be very hard to ever completely forget such things.

But you can forgive.

You can get rid of the rawness of the pain.

You can release the memory so it no longer controls your emotions, reactions, and thoughts.

If you have been the victim of sexual abuse, physical abuse, or childhood emotional abuse or neglect, I am truly sorry for the pain you have suffered. I hurt with you. But you will never find peace and freedom from the perpetrator of a crime against you until you are able to forgive that individual. Remember, forgiving the offender in no way excuses that person for the harm he or she has caused you, but it will release you from the continuing power of resentment and bitterness.

One word of caution: in releasing and forgiving an offender, it is not always possible, nor advisable, for you to go back physically to the one who hurt you and speak with him or her face to face. The person may live a long way away, or you may not know where he or she is anymore. The offender may have died. Or maybe it could just be physically or emotionally harmful for you to see and speak to this person again.

What do you do in those kinds of situations? Here are two suggestions:

The Empty Chair

You get an empty chair, imagine the offender seated there, and tell him or her what you feel. You may say something like, "I need to say some things to you. You hurt me . . . " And then you spell out your hurt. *How* did the person hurt you? Say something like, "You hurt me this way, this way, and this way."

Then forgive the person. Tell the offender, "I want you to know I forgive you, because resentment isn't working, and it's keeping me stuck in the process of becoming more like Jesus. God has forgiven me, and because I want forgiveness in the future, I am forgiving and releasing you."

Say it to the chair.

The Unsent Letter

Put your hurt down in black and white. You've been carrying it so long, you need to unload it, and you can let it out in a letter. Write down all you want to say to your offender, and then at the end say something like, "But starting today, I forgive you, because resentment doesn't work. God has forgiven me, and because I want forgiveness in the future, I am forgiving and releasing you."

Never mail the letter.

Burn it, throw it away, or keep it safely tucked away as a memento of your decision to forgive. If you ever find your anger rising again, reread the letter (or rewrite it) and remind yourself that you canceled the debt.

Do it for your own sake—but do it. Release the offender so you can get a fresh start.

Moving Forward in Release

Please know that forgiving people is tough for even the most mature of Christ-followers. I know people whom I greatly respect in their spiritual journeys who can still name the people who have offended them. Their memories still trigger anger, resentment, and pain. They're still carrying a grudge. So don't think this is simple. Even as a pastor, when someone hurts me, I don't say, "Praise the Lord! I forgive you, O blessed one; let's have tea and crumpets." There are times when I get furious. I'm over-whelmed by thoughts of hatred and vengeance.

Forgiving is real work—and it's costly. It cost God His only Son. It cost Jesus His life. And forgiving will cost *you*. And the biggest cost to forgiveness is your pride. Whenever you forgive, you let go of your right to hold on to a grudge, prove the person wrong, and win. But if you are going to be obedient, you must sacrifice what you want for what God wants for you. Here's the heart of this message: God's not asking you to forgive your offenders because they deserve His forgiveness; He's ask-ing you to forgive them because He has forgiven you—and you *don't* deserve forgiveness.

So I write this as an encouragement to forgive, and keep on forgiv-ing. It's the only way forward. It's an instrumental step toward a fresh start. Each time you forgive, you release a prisoner—and then find out the prisoner was actually you. You were in bondage to anger, resent-ment, and bitterness. Forgiveness is the action of cooperation with the Holy Spirit that sets you free.

When forgiveness becomes a habit in your life, something inside of you comes alive. That's abundant living. My prayer is that you'll replace the "I can't do it" with "I will cancel the debt," and see what God will do in your life. He wants the very best for you! Just watch what happens when you're obedient to Him.

CHAPTER 6

CONFLICT: AN UNIMAGINED ADVENTURE

Recently I was unable to attend the final game of my son's baseball tournament. The game was really important to me since I've coached most of his teams and rarely miss games, so I asked my wife to capture everything on camera so I could enjoy it later.

Now, I'm not a professional photographer by any means, but photography is enough of a hobby for me that we've invested some decent money to own some good equipment. To make a long story painful—when my sweet wife left the baseball field, she forgot our camera bag containing my camera, multiple lenses, and our video recorder.

We didn't even realize this blunder until two days later when I went to look for the camera bag and it wasn't around: thousands of dollars of equipment was simply gone. The video of my son's championship baseball game was also gone. Gone was the recording of his eighth-grade graduation, which was also in the bag—the video where he did a full-on dance as he got his diploma, a priceless family treasure lost forever.

You should have seen the fireworks in my house. Whoa, baby! Anger, frustration, hurtful words—it got a little ugly.

Wouldn't it be great if everybody got along with one another all the time? Yeah, well, not on this planet! Conflicts happen. Put any two people together—even two people who love each other a lot—and sooner or later they're bound to disagree on something or get angry with one another. My wife and I love each other. No question about that. But we certainly had a conflict over forgetting to bring the equipment home. It was a loss, and loss is painful.

Think of a current conflict in your life—perhaps one that isn't resolved yet. What does that conflict feel like to you?

I doubt that anyone truly enjoys conflict. Some people say they thrive on conflict, but I think they simply enjoy the rush of adrenaline that conflict inevitably brings. Even divorce lawyers or investigative reporters—people who make their living from entering into conflict on a regular basis—say unresolved conflict is hard to live with for extended times. No sane person wakes up in the morning, fists clenched, and says, "Yes! Another day to be alive and in turmoil with people!"

The problem with conflict is that it's easy to allow it to go unresolved. These unresolved issues tend to eat away at us and grow and fester, sapping our strength and bubbling underneath the surface of our lives. Something will trigger a memory of the disagreement, and the hurt boils up anew. It's so easy to relive the pain of a conflict again and again.

Spiritually, it's difficult to continue to grow in faith when we're stuck in a conflict. There's a very close correlation between our relationship with God and our relationship with others. When something is out of whack with people, our connection with God usually suffers as well. Living with unresolved conflict is not reflective of the abundant life God promised. It's not how God intended us to live.

So what do we do? If we feel stuck because of an unresolved quarrel, how do we get going again? How do we move from stuck to a fresh start?

A Troubling Word

Think about the last time you didn't get along with someone. Was it with your spouse? Your kids? Your boss? Your parents? A friend? A neighbor? If the conflict is still not settled, there's a good chance it's eating away at you right now.

Personally, I hate conflict. Even the word *conflict* sounds painful! It has a harsh ring to it. The etymology of the word involves the prefix *con-* and the suffix *-flict*. *Con-* is from the same source from which we developed the word *constipation*. And *-flict* is the origin of *afflicted*, as in, *What a drag! I'm afflicted with constipation.* (Okay, I haven't really fact-checked all that, but that's the image I get when I think of conflict—*constipated affliction*.)

I can't stand the feeling I get when I experience tension with others. Conflict causes me more bodily stress than anything I do. People think it's stressful to speak to crowds, and it can be. But I'd rather speak to a million people than experience tension with just one—especially someone I care about.

Whenever I have conflict with the people I'm closest to—ouch! I want it resolved right away so that I don't have to live with *that* feeling. And if it can't be fixed immediately, I just want to run away, cover my ears, and sing "la-la-la-la-la." Conflict tends to produce physical consequences in me. I obsess over it. I play and replay scenarios in my mind. It eats away at my stomach. I can't sleep. I tend to drink a lot of Diet Coke and eat too many Doritos, so I end up gassy . . . and bloated . . . which is how I came up with the aforementioned meaning of conflict. The bottom line is, whenever I'm in conflict, I'm completely devoid of peace.

Can you relate to those feelings? Think about it:

» Conflict and fear are closely related. Whenever you don't get along with someone, you fear what will result. You fear being around that person; you fear the tension that can crop up again, anytime. You fear the future.

» Conflict and loss are closely related. Unless a conflict is resolved, you will probably lose something—a relationship, an opportunity, a job, a good performance review, a contract, a marriage.

» Conflict and pain are closely related. Conflicts hurt relationally, emotionally, physically, and spiritually. No one enjoys pain.

But here's some surprising news—and this is what I'd like to focus on throughout the rest of this chapter: in spite of all the fear, loss, and pain associated with conflict, it can actually be a good thing.

How?

Conflict Can Be Used for a Good Purpose

Believe it or not, conflict can actually be part of God's strategy to transform us into the people He wants us to be. God can use the conflict in our lives for His glory. In brief, conflict can be part of God's adventure for us.

That's the new paradigm I want to suggest you consider. Conflict is closely linked to adventure—God's adventure. Now, I realize that when I think of conflict with another person, the word that *doesn't* automatically come to mind is adventure. So let's unpack this concept some more.

An adventure is usually an event filled with good excitement, the kind that challenges you beyond what you previously thought capable. For instance, an adventure is a missions trip where you go build houses in the hot Tijuana sun. Or a camping trip where you see a bear eat your cookies and you run up a tree and live to tell about it.

So how can relational conflict possibly be an adventure? Think of it this way: the one factor present in all adventures is conflict. In order to have an adventure, you need some sort of obstacle to overcome. If you didn't have an obstacle, there would be no challenge. The adventure would be boring. And no one ever has a boring adventure. It's impossible. You can't have an adventure while sitting on your couch, eating cereal. Unless, of course, you choke on your Lucky Charms, and paramedics rush to your aid.

Whenever we're involved in a conflict, we're forced to overcome an obstacle. And in dealing with that obstacle, we're invited to seek Christ more intensely. That's when the adventure truly begins—when the conflict drives us to our knees. In the midst of the conflict, we encounter a situation that is so unclear, difficult, and tension filled, that we need a good Guide to navigate the path. This is where Jesus comes in. Smack-dab in the middle of our battle, He joins us and offers us a clear light to the other side. Think of Jesus walking out on the water to Peter in the midst of a storm (Mark 6:45–52). With water raging all around him, Peter is offered a new glimpse into a life of faith. He would never have received that opportunity if he had not been out in a storm.

That's our invitation in the middle of conflict: to see any such struggle as an invitation to Christ's adventure in transformation. Christ extends His hand to us and invites us to walk with Him through the storm. As we seek Him, He transforms us into deeper, richer, and more meaningful people. Conflict is the catalyst that God uses to show Himself to us and to cause new growth to happen in our lives.

But we are never to seek conflict for conflict's sake alone. We aren't called to jump into the middle of hairy situations simply to test God's goodness and guidance for our lives. But as we seek to walk with Him in the normal scope of life, conflict inevitably happens. In fact, in Hebrews 12:14, God offers His plan for managing conflict: "Make every effort to live in peace with all men and to be holy."

So, how do we "make every effort"? I'm going to share with you a practical way to cooperate with Christ in the adventure of conflict. And I've written an easy little jingle to help you remember how:

Ouch!—What?—Who?—What?

Say that jingle out loud wherever you are while reading this book. I know . . . the coffee shop crowd may already think you're nuts. (Remember in chapter 5 when you called the stranger next to you messy?) But it doesn't matter. Here you go again.

The above jingle is shorthand for a fresh start when it comes to conflict. When you learn what it means, and apply it to your life, you can begin to deal with conflict in a healthy way. If you're someone who values peace and also values relationships, you'll want to figure this out so conflict doesn't become a roadblock to God's life for you.

Let's take a look at what each word means:

Ouch!

"Ouch!" means we're hurt, and we need to get on the road to peace.

Some people are masters at sensing when something is wrong, and they don't need conflict pointed out. The conflict could be expressed as a simple raised eyebrow from another person, a tone, a pause in a statement, an unusual word, a mysterious black eye, a middle finger . . . whatever. You sense the "ouch" quickly and move to your reactionary mode.

Others are less adept at sensing when something is wrong and often need to be clued in to the conflict around them. If you're this way, someone could flip you off and you'll think, *Nice nails*.

Most of us fall somewhere in between. Regardless, whenever there's conflict, we resort to our default mode of reacting to conflict, and that's either learned or based on a preferred personality style. Let's consider some stereotypical actions—these are also known as "conflict management" styles. See if one of these describes your default mode when there's a situation:

1. You grow angry. You're ticked and others around you know it. You're quick to react and blame. That vein in your neck pulsates. Unkind words often flow from your mouth. You are quick to respond and take action in conflict. Sometimes that action is negative.

2. You stew. This is when conflict causes silence. When something's wrong, you retreat, back off, distance yourself from others . . . you basically sit and simmer. If someone asks you what's wrong, you say, "Nothing." (This is my reaction style, by the way.)

3. You deny it. If there's tension, you say, "What tension? There's nothing wrong." You keep going as if that statement were true. But there is something wrong. You just don't acknowledge the truth of the situation.

4. You swipe silently. This reactionary style is similar to denial, but it goes a step further. On the surface, your first response to conflict is to deny it. It's life as usual, all smiles. But when the person is not looking, you stab him in the back . . . *bam!* This is often referred to as the *passive-aggressive* approach.

Which of the above responses comes the closest to describing you?

Okay, now, regardless of your typical reaction style, I want to move on to acknowledge something important. At this "ouch" stage, you take a deep breath and realize something big . . .

Conflict hurts.

This is the "ouch" component. Conflict happens, and we all react in various ways. But regardless of how we react, the healthy thing to do is realize the pain connected to the situation. We must also realize that we live in a broken world.

The Bible states this plainly. Romans 3:23 says, "For all have sinned; all fall short of God's glorious standard" (NLT). Conflict happens because of sin and free will. It's part of the world that God has allowed; He has given us free choice. In fact, conflict goes back to the very beginning of the Bible. You have Cain and Abel—two brothers who disagreed over obedience issues, and then one killed the other. There were only a handful of people on earth at the time and already there was jealousy, deception, conflict, and the first murder in history. Humanity was off to a rousing start!

Surprisingly, part of the good journey God invites us on involves acknowledging the pain of conflict. When we do this, we are more freely able to resolve to seek peace. We don't want to be in pain anymore, and we don't want discord to damage our relationships. So when the "ouch" happens, we acknowledge it for what it is. This first step is an important one as we move down the right pathway.

In simplest terms, whenever an "ouch" happens, our invitation is to realize that (1) the world is broken, (2) conflict hurts, and (3) we want to live at peace regardless.

What?

"What?" asks, "What hurt?" and "What was my part in causing that?"

This is my least favorite of the actions. This first *What?* means that I need to identify either my pain or my insensitivity. Psalm 4:4 tells us directly to take this inner look: "In your anger do not sin; when you are on your beds, search your hearts and be silent."

This challenge isn't easy. It requires us to hold up a magnifying mirror to our lives and go looking for something bigger than the apparent blackheads. When we take this action, we must search our inner lives to figure out the roots of pain (ouch!).

The first question to ask after acknowledging the pain of a conflict is simply, "What hurt me?"

Perhaps it was one of these things:

» Your normal routine was disrupted by a situation someone threw at you.
» Your neighbor got something you want.

» Somebody said or did something that belittled or disrespected you.

» You were made to look stupid or unimportant in front of others.

» Something you've accomplished was devalued.

» People don't accept you.

» You reached out and were rejected.

» Someone you care about doesn't seem to care about you anymore.

Why is it so important to define what hurt? First, whenever I can articulate my feelings, I move one step closer to peace. There's nothing very helpful in saying things such as, "I don't know . . . stuff just hurts," and leaving it at that. Second, sometimes I discover that my hurt is about something askew in my life. I experience conflict, not because of what another person did or said, but because my own issues allowed the conflict to surface.

For instance, last Fourth of July, I got angry at one of my kids because I didn't feel I was getting enough help in preparing for a family party. So I started making snappy comments, and my child snapped back, and pretty soon it turned into a verbal joust where I was called names that only a child can get away with.

So then I was hurt, and I swiftly moved into my default mode: I stewed. And my stew soon turned into a pout. I was in real danger of letting this conflict get me stuck.

But here's where I turned the corner. While in this pout, I acknowledged my hurt. I said, "Ouch!" so to speak, and then started to ask the *What?* questions—I began to define my hurt.

As I held up the mirror to my inner life, I realized that I was hurt because I was facing my own fear as a parent. I was struggling with the fact that my child[1] is a teenager now, and maybe I haven't done my job as a parent to prepare this child to survive in the real world. That child's work ethic isn't where it should be to survive. And I love my children too much to not prepare them.

My real conflict was not about how fast the back patio was being swept.

It was about me.

My hurt was rooted in my fear and insecurity as a parent. Like a dummy, I had lashed out in blame to pacify my hurt.

If the first question in *What?* is to ask what hurt, the second part is, "What was my part in causing this 'ouch'?" What did I do (or not do) to initiate or further the conflict? What was my role in causing unnecessary pain? What did I say or not say? Was there a particular tone, a look, anything that contributed to what happened?

Typically, we don't spend much time with this question because we want to swiftly move to blame others, which helps us justify our actions and minimize our part in the pain. But the key here is to go beyond our actions and look at our motives. Actions are easy to define. I yelled, I swore, I gossiped, whatever. But motive is the biggie. We are complex people and have mixed motives for nearly everything we do. And God cares deeply about our motives. Proverbs 16:2 puts this into perspective: "People may be pure in their own eyes, but the LORD examines their motives" (NLT).

What does it require for us to examine our motives? It takes time, sincere reflection, and brutal honesty to see why we really do what we do.

Who?

"Who?" asks, "Who is involved?"

If we want to get to the deeper issues connected with conflict, we must stop and recognize that when the conflict-bomb exploded, shrapnel went flying and others were probably wounded in the midst of the clash. Sometimes the wounded are innocent. When we ask the question, *Who?* we are able to see the scope of the discord. This question identifies those involved.

For example, when I have an argument with my wife, there may be three other observers to this tension: my children. They aren't oblivious to an argument, and they probably experience some collateral damage. Even if my anger isn't directed at them, it can wound them by creating fear. I need to consider that.

Or if I have a conflict with a coworker, I may need to stop and realize that he will probably take our conflict home, putting a strain on his marriage. We might call this "conflict dominoes." My domino falls and trips his, and then his falls and trips his wife's, his wife's trips the kids[1] . . . and the next thing you know, the cat is flying through the window (although landing on its feet and looking for a mouse to damage).

Now, I can't be responsible if a coworker goes home and chooses to act like an idiot with his family. But if I'm an idiot with him first, I need to realize that my idiocy has potential to begin the domino effect.

Why care about how others respond when they're not around us? Because if we are on a journey with Jesus, then we are called to love others (Luke 10:27). Loving others means we care about collateral damage. As Philippians 2:3–4 tells us, "Don't be selfish. . . . Don't think only about your own affairs, but be interested in others, too" (NLT).

When we ask, "Who is involved in conflict?" this lets us see the scale of what's taken place. It's another step forward in the good adventure of being a follower of Jesus.

What?

"What?" is asking, "What is needed?"

Notice this second *What?* and final action is not, "What do I want to do?" Most people want to do one of two things when it comes to conflict: (1) people either want to be *liked*, or (2) people want to be proven *right*. I usually find myself in the first group—I want to be liked (I also want to be right . . . just not as much as I want to be liked). Because of that, you know what I typically want to do with conflict? Whatever leads to the least amount of relational pain. I don't have to be right, but I do have to be liked.

I can almost guarantee that every time you deal with conflict in a healthy way, it's going to be difficult. This last *What?* is about doing what is right, not what is easy.

What's right is to seek peace. We can't control the response of others, but we can control our actions and make every effort as a follower of Jesus to do what leads to peace.

What does this look like? Well, to live in peace, I may need to do my utmost to *confront, apologize,* and *forgive.*

Confront

I realize some of us would rather die than confront. But a confrontation doesn't have to be synonymous with a battle. Not if the confrontation is rooted in humility and gentleness, and there's a genuine desire for peace.

Confrontation that leads to peace isn't about domination; it's about a conversation. The apostle Paul made an interesting statement when he talked about confronting his friend and fellow believer Peter: "When Peter came to Antioch, I opposed him to his face, because he was clearly in the wrong" (Gal. 2:11). When possible, have a face-to-face *conversation.* Don't use e-mail or the phone. A face-to-face conversation lets you share what you realized in step two (what hurt?). It lets you say to the other person: (1) here's what hurt me, and (2) this is what I see as my part in our conflict. And it allows you to gauge reaction.

It's important to recognize any part you may share in a conflict. Perhaps you were tired. Perhaps you were misunderstood. Perhaps you overreacted. (These are not excuses but factors—pieces of the puzzle.) In Matthew 7:3 Jesus provided us with a word picture to help us see that no one is above error: "Why do you notice the little piece of dust in your friend's eye, but you don't notice the big piece of wood in your own eye?" (NCV).

There's a word for telling other people their faults without dealing honestly with our own: hypocrisy. We are hypocrites if we confront others without first confronting ourselves.

Apologize

Adults are great at teaching children to say they're sorry: "Hey, you apologize to your sister for hitting her in the face with the spatula." This action is much more difficult when you're older. Most people I know don't like to apologize without some form of prompting.

But think about it: what does an apology cost you? Nothing! Well, nothing really important. It does cost you your pride. But pride is a good thing to give up. Pride is like fool's gold: we're fools if we think it's valuable. In the grand scheme of life, pride is worthless. It's more than worthless actually; it's costly. The more pride we hang on to, the less we'll experience God's favor and blessing. The book of Proverbs teaches us, "Pride leads to disgrace, but with humility comes wisdom. . . . Pride ends in humiliation, while humility brings honor" (11:2; 29:23 NLT).

One more thought here: apologize carefully. You don't need to apologize for everything and anything. To apologize for godly actions and reactions, however misunderstood, is sin. It's naming as sin something that is not sin, and that's a sin in itself. Apologize specifically for where you were wrong. Only that.

Forgive

Forgiveness is like that vitamin E oil that is supposed to make scars heal better. Anytime we extend forgiveness to someone who has wronged us, a scar is minimized. If we don't extend forgiveness, our wounds don't heal and are opened every time we remember the conflict.

I'll be honest: forgiveness is a very difficult step, as we saw in the previous chapter. When I'm hurt in a conflict, my first response isn't to forgive. I don't run to the kitchen to bake a reconciliation cake. No, my flesh wants to hurt the other person. I want a meteor to strike him. I want to smile at his pain and pray silently that he experiences something similar to what he caused me. I want to take the candles off the cake and burn down his house—okay, that's a little extreme—but I definitely want the meteor to strike. I want revenge!

But those feelings I have are not motivated by God's Spirit. They are my natural feelings, and they don't please God. Spiritual maturity drives me to forgive. A fresh start is dependent on it. To do what it takes to live at peace, I have to forgive regardless of the difficulty.

Jesus felt and understood pain, betrayal, and conflict. But He modeled forgiveness. When He was brutally nailed to the cross, He prayed this prayer for those who had put Him there: "Forgive them; for they know not what they do" (Luke 23:34 KJV). A fresh start requires that we follow His actions.

On the Road to Peace Today

Conflict is a fact of life. It happens to all of us. But it doesn't need to keep us stuck. In fact, conflict can be an adventure—*if* Christ is guiding our lives. Remember, Christ invites us to live life to the fullest. He wants us to thrive and grow. But spiritual growth doesn't come about by avoiding conflict; rather, it occurs when we handle conflict by cooperating with God's instructions. The goal in this process isn't always to reconcile a relationship. A relationship may be too damaged, or a person may be downright dangerous. The goal is peace. Make *every* effort to live in peace, and watch God take your conflict and use it to transform you into who He wants you to be—for His glory. That's an adventure beyond imagination!

CHAPTER 7

TO BOLDLY GO

Have you ever noticed that the human race is made up of two kinds of people? There are those who live, breathe, dress, and act *Star Trek*—and those who absolutely despise it. If you're in the latter category, my apologies up front for this first illustration. But bear with me—there is a point. And it isn't to invite you to the next national *Star Trek* convention with me. I promise.

Star Trek centers around a futuristic group of people in outer space on a mission to explore the universe. Their mission is summarized in a famous line that almost everyone knows, even those who hate the show: *To boldly go where no man has gone before.*

The people of *Star Trek* were not just going—they were *boldly* going. And that one little word can make all the difference when what you want is a fresh start.

You see, as we journey through life, it's very easy to lapse into what I like to call "survival mode." This is where our mission becomes clouded. We're not sure what God is calling us to. Maybe we are weary or grieving, have unmet goals, or simply don't feel like we have energy to go beyond life's basics, such as eating, sleeping, feeding the cat, and watching reruns of *Star Trek*. But I'm guessing that anyone who's reading a book titled *Fresh Start* isn't interested in living life in survival mode. You want a new perspective for starting anew. You want to go through life boldly. You're not content with what you already know, what you can already do, and who you already are. You want growth and action and passion and mastery, and you want to be challenged. You crave a life beyond what you're experiencing now. And that longing is very precious to God—because He put it there.

This longing shows up in the smallest kids. When our firstborn was an infant, she quickly mastered the words "No, me." Thousands of times she said it. She didn't want Mommy and Daddy's help with anything. She wanted to do it on her own. To live boldly. If we tried to help her into her car seat, put a toy together for her, help her ride her tricycle— anything!—she'd announce, "No, *me!*" (I can't relate. Whenever she had a dirty diaper, I'd yelp—"No, *Mom*.")

As children, most of us experience a similar drive to live boldly. We push to drink deeply from all that life has to offer. Yet as we get older, that drive often gets wiped out by a killer disease called discouragement. Discouragement can become a cancer to the soul. It destroys dreams. It's a thief to living life the way God intended life to be lived. Boldly.

Is discouragement prevalent in your life? If so, there is a hope. Discouragement is a natural part of life's journey, but Jesus Christ invites you to move out of the swamp of discouragement and into a bright place of hope. He doesn't want you to be stuck in discouragement any longer. He came to give you a fresh start!

More Common than You Think

It's true: everyone experiences discouragement from time to time. Nobody can entirely dismiss it. It's one of the emotions God allows us to experience. If things have happened that have made us feel discouraged, it's okay to feel that way. For a while anyway.

The problem comes when discouragement becomes a way of life. Or when we're too easily discouraged. Or we're discouraged all the time. Or we can't remember when we didn't feel discouraged. Actually, I'll make a strong statement: I think discouragement can be worse than depression at times (key phrase: *at times*). At least with depression, we can seek help and get a diagnosis. But discouragement can be more insidious because it's so easy to hide. It can become a slow growing mold that creeps into all the corners of our lives and spreads pessimism and negativity over everything we do.

Have you ever met a person who doesn't appear to be discouraged, but you strongly suspect he is? Often, this kind of person is a Christian who sincerely loves God. Unfortunately, he believes that God is anti-discouragement, so he shouldn't feel this way.

"How's it going?" you ask.

He turns on a giant happy face and exclaims: "Special!" There's a pause while he musters chipperness, and it's full steam ahead: "It's a beautiful day, and everything is cheery, and I love Mister Rogers, and my smile could stop the fighting in the Middle East. One look at me and all those insurgents and terrorists would just drop their weapons and sing, 'God Is So Good.'"

I have just one request for those kinds of Christians . . . *stop!*

It doesn't help to mask discouragement with cheeriness, or to pretend it doesn't exist, or to hide behind platitudes of positive spiritual thinking. Discouragement happens. God invites us to truth and authenticity about it. He also invites us not to stay there.

What happens when we do stay stuck in discouragement? Let's talk about a couple of big ways that it can damage us:

Discouragement Sidetracks Us

A couple years ago, *USA Today* did a story on a homeless alcoholic in New York City who boldly saved a woman named Sonya Lopez and her two-year-old son. Their house was on fire, and they were trapped inside. The homeless man, named John Byrnes, talked the woman into throwing her son down to him on the street below. Byrnes caught the twenty-seven-pound boy, and then helped Sonya get out. The child was uninjured, and his mother was treated for smoke inhalation and released. Both are doing fine.

Later, when Byrnes was interviewed, he characterized himself as "a drunken bum." Then, in a discouraged tone, he said he would always be one.

I wonder, did Sonya Lopez think of John Byrnes as a drunken bum? To her, he was a certified hero. Even in his drunken stupor, he did something bold and honorable. But John Byrnes had been discouraged for so long that he could no longer see how worthy he was in God's eyes. That's how long-term discouragement can affect us. It can sidetrack us from our true mission.

Maybe you're saying, *Come on, Doug . . . that's kind of a radical illustration. My discouragement hasn't led me to live on the streets.*

Well, what about the so-called *lesser* bouts of discouragement, the ones that might not turn us into alcoholics, but still

» impact our moods, keeping us critical, cynical, negative, or pessimistic?
» affect our relationships?
» make us tough to be around?
» steal our joy?

» keep us from celebrating?

» makes us anxious?

» prevent us from ever feeling satisfied?

If any of these ring a bell, then there's a good chance you're stuck in discouragement. And, as in other stuck areas, God offers a new start.

Discouragement Makes Us More Vulnerable to Temptation

Whenever we're discouraged, our emotional barriers are low and we're more likely to give in to temptation. Think about it. What sorts of temptation are you more prone to giving in to when you're discouraged? Maybe you have said something to yourself (either consciously or subconsciously) like this:

» "My beet and prune juice and tree-bark cereal diet just isn't cutting it. I haven't even lost a pound!"—so you eat the whole box of Krispy Kreme donuts.

» "I feel so down right now. I need *something* to pick me up."—as you click on an inappropriate Web site.

» "I can't *stand* what I'm going through. I'm *so* mad!"—and you hit your spouse, kick the cat, or punch your fist through the wall.

Often, when you're discouraged, familiar words of rationalization come to mind—four very destructive words—"I might as well." I might as well eat that, drink that, give in to that, read that, watch that, buy that, steal that, lie about that . . . the list is never ending. Then, when you do give in to the temptation, you feel worse and get even more discouraged, so you do it all over again. It's a vicious and painful cycle, and it keeps you from really living the best life God has for you.

Are you brave enough to admit that you get discouraged more often than you'd like? If so, you're not alone.

In Good Company

If you're feeling discouraged, take heart—you're in good company. The Scriptures are full of stories of men and women who experienced discouragement along life's journey. Have you ever read the Psalms? There are several different types of psalms: thanksgiving psalms, royal psalms about kings, and psalms of wisdom. But the number one category is psalms of *lament*—a fancy word for "articulated discouragement." Think about it: the most frequent type of psalm in the Bible is about voicing discouragement to God. No wonder it's the most popular book in the Bible—it connects with people where they are.

Consider the words of Psalm 142. David wrote:

> *I cry aloud to the LORD;*
> *I lift up my voice to the LORD for mercy.*
> *I pour out my complaint before him;*
> *before him I tell my trouble. . . .*
> *In the path where I walk*
> *men have hidden a snare for me.*
> *Look to my right and see;*
> *no one is concerned for me.*
> *I have no refuge;*
> *no one cares for my life. (vv. 1–4)*

When David recorded these words, he was in a place of deep discouragement. At one time in his life he had everything going for him, but it all fell apart. He found himself on the run, hiding in a cave, scraping bat guano off his sandals, and crying out to God.

Maybe you're at a similar place in your life. What do you do? Let's look at two big questions that arise in studying this topic: (1) How can we learn from discouragement? (2) How can we limit discouragement?

How Can We Learn from Discouragement?

Learning from discouragement involves some inner reflection. So, in order to go after a fresh start, let's do some very practical work in this area right now. Take a moment to read through the four questions below. After each question and the commentary that follows, write your own answer in the spaces provided.

What Kinds of Things Regularly Discourage Me?

Triggers for discouragement follow common themes, everyday situations involving the people and places in our day-to-day lives. For example, in my own life, I'm often discouraged when I'm surrounded by clutter. This may seem trivial to you, but I get really down when our house is messy. Normally our house is tidy, but when things get out of whack, that seems to trigger a melancholy mood.

Another trigger for me is when my kids are mean to one another in the car. Whenever it happens, my first response isn't anger; it's discouragement. I get sad. I so badly want them to treat each other better.

I also get discouraged when I let people down, those times when I'm not being the type of person, friend, employee, coach, spouse, parent, or pastor I need to be. For instance, every Thanksgiving Day my friend and I have a tradition of running the Turkey Trot race in Dana Point, California. (Actually, I jog it . . . running indicates actual speed.) Last time, it didn't go so well—we were both supposed to show up in shape to run. He was. I wasn't. As the race began, I was hobbling along, and my buddy kept saying things like, "Don't worry about it; I'm fine going slow." Then he's running backward . . . doing jumping jacks while he circles me. Things went from bad to worse: little kids started running between my legs; senior citizens with walkers started zooming by. There was a turtle in there somewhere too, I'm sure. And I felt discouraged. Why? I let my friend down by not being better prepared.

Okay, that was a brief peek at some discouragement triggers on my list. What's on yours? Take a few moments to write your answers below.

I feel discouraged when:

_____

_____

_____

Why Am I *Really* Discouraged Right Now?

This question prompts us to go deeper. It invites us to take the items on the list we just made and ask, "What's underneath them?"

I know, some of you counselor types have already figured out my clutter issue and are having your own little therapy session with my life. I know . . . I'm a control freak, perfectionist, manic. Whatever. Let me save you the official diagnosis. I know I'm whacked. I understand it. I'm working on it. Thank you very much. (Not as crazy as the therapists, though . . . you know what I mean.)

How about the issue of discouragement when my kids are mean to one another? Why am I discouraged when that happens? The answer to the why is that I'm afraid it's my fault. I'm not the dad I should be. I think about all the things I should have done as a dad . . . and if I had done those things, we'd all be more loving, and God would be glorified, and we'd be the perfect pastor's family . . . in Fantasyland.

So let's ask some *why* questions right now. If you don't ask the *why* question, you'll end up living your life on the surface, never getting to the root reason for your discouragement. There's always something there when you dig a little deeper—but it's often too difficult to do, and people give up—and discouragement continues to win.

Take a few moments and jot down your answers below.

The reason I'm really discouraged is:

_____

_____

_____

What Might God Say to Me Through Scripture Now?

In the midst of discouragement, this question can feel counterintuitive to what we feel. We feel bad, so we can't imagine anything positive. Yet it's very important to ask this question, because God's Word provides the healing surgery needed.

For instance, if I'm discouraged because my kids are acting up, and I realize that it's because I'm afraid, then I need to find out what God has to say about fear. I could then find a hundred Scriptures that tell me, "Fear not," "Don't be afraid," and "Be courageous" (NLT).

I know some will think, *Good for you, Pastor—you know the Bible. But when I'm discouraged, I'm not racing to read my Bible. I'm racing to the refrigerator.* I understand. I don't always turn immediately to Scripture either. When I'm discouraged, I'm thinking about me first, and at times the Scriptures can seem dry and difficult to discern.

That's why we need God's Word planted in our hearts ahead of time. Then, when we're discouraged, we can hold fast to what we know about God and cling to His words. This is when we remember in the dark what we learned in the light.

So, what is a verse that might apply to your specific area of discouragement? If you can't think of one, e-mail your pastor or a trusted friend, or search under "God's promises" on the Internet, and you should be able to find something. Pray that God will bring just the right verses to mind.

A verse that applies to how I'm feeling is:

_____

_____

_____

Where Do I Need to Change?

There is a positive side to discouragement. It teaches us about ourselves. Discouragement reveals unfulfilled hopes and expectations, and also reveals areas where God needs to change our lives. If we pay heed, discouragement doesn't have to win. But remember that, as with anything else, we have to *cooperate* with God when He reveals those areas that need change. He, of course, has the power; now we have to do our part. Stay close to God. Pray. Then move in the direction of your prayers.

How might we cooperate with God so that we defeat discouragement? Here are a few suggestions:

A change of scenery. Sometimes our circumstances create discouragement, so an external change is helpful. Paint a room, start volunteering in a ministry, move your desk into the sunnier part of the office, or get out of the house.

A change of peeps. Discouragement is contagious! So limit your exposure to people who are always down in the dumps. Some people love to find others to commiserate with them. Do you know anyone like this? Turn tail and run!

I know what I just wrote sounds harsh, so listen carefully: if you know people who live their lives constantly discouraged, yes, love them, spend time with them, minister to them—but don't get joined at the hip. If people are sucking you into their discouragement vortex, you have to change something. You must limit anything and anyone who pulls you away from God. Jesus did this. He ministered to everyone, but He also regularly withdrew from crowds and chose carefully with whom He would hang out.

A change in our inner world. We may need to look past others and examine—and change—our own thought patterns, attitudes, and responses. For instance, when my kids acted out in the car, my instinct was instantly to yell at them. It was ineffective, threatening, and demeaning. A typical situation went like this:

Me to kids: "Look—you guys knock it off. If I have to pull this car over, I'll give you something to yell about."

Them to me: "Something to yell about? Hmmm . . . Does that mean you're going to take us to a baseball game, Dad?"

Yelling seldom works. It never worked when my parents yelled at my sisters and me for acting up in the car. They never actually pulled the car over, and neither will I. At least not on the freeways of Los Angeles.

In a situation like this, I have to change the focus of my hope. To hope that my kids will never be mean to one another is unrealistic. I need to change from hoping *they'll* be perfect to hoping *I* can help them learn and grow from their conflict.

So now I take their hurtful comments and turn them into bedtime curricula. When I go to tuck them in, I sit on the side of their beds and talk to them about relationships, family, and values. It's a more positive approach. I may not stop all the fighting in the car, but at least now I'll avoid discouragement, because I changed something about myself.

How Can We Limit Discouragement?

Let me suggest some ways that we can limit discouragement. Some of these actions are relatively simple; others are more difficult to implement. All are part of the overall plan to cooperate with the direction God is moving us.

Schedule Leisure

The idea of planning leisure sounds like a bit of an oxymoron. But the truth is that we are morons when we don't have any downtime in our lives. If you're a busy person, no one will hand you leisure. You have to schedule it into your life, or it will never happen.

God wired us to need leisure. That's why He created the Sabbath and commanded a day of rest. It's so important that God even rested Himself (Gen. 2:2–3). So why shouldn't we?

Very rarely do we hear about life's pace being connected to discouragement, but I think there's a big connection. When we don't get enough rest, we deplete our energy. And when our energy is low, we're more prone to discouragement. We must be ruthless with our calendars in order to find leisure and say no to busyness.

Practice Encouragement

There's something refreshing about people who consistently encourage others. They seem to be in a different class than the rest of us. Their discouragement is minimal in comparison. I don't have stats to support that. It's just my intuitive observation.

Proverbs 11:25 puts a surprising twist on things. It says, "He who refreshes others will himself be refreshed." That means that while the spoken word has such incredible effect on the people who hear it, it also has a powerful impact on those who deliver it. Whenever you encourage others, it lifts your discouragement. Ephesians 4:29 says, "Let everything you say be good and helpful, so that your words will be an encouragement to those who hear them" (NLT). Why does God give us directives like that? Because He knows they're in our best interest.

Encouragement is a habit that can be developed. Try to do it every day so it can become part of your vocabulary, part of your life, and eventually a reflection of your spirit. It can be a difficult habit to develop at first, and may even feel a little forced. You might wonder what to say: "Uh . . . well . . . nice shirt, and, uh . . . you don't sweat much."

Good start. Check it off—day one. Pick it up again tomorrow and after a while you will become an all-star encourager. Soon it will be natural and you'll be leaving encouraging voicemails and notes and giving face-to-face words of encouragement. You'll also limit your own discouragement by encouraging others. It's a law of nature: you can't focus on your inner "ugly" if you're looking for outside beauty. You can't be whiny and winsome at the same time.

Another angle with this encouragement concept is to develop an "encouragement" file. When you get nice letters or something encouraging, don't delete them or throw them away—file them. That way, whenever you're discouraged, you can open the file and be reminded of the good stuff in your life. Encouragement works when it's received too.

Pray about the Source of Your Discouragement

This has been very helpful to me. When someone or something discourages me, I try to make that person or thing the object of my prayer. That's actually biblical. Jesus said, "Pray for those who persecute you" (Matt. 5:44). So that's what I try to do. If some person is causing me discouragement, I ask God to bless him or her, and He heals the pain there. It actually changes *my* attitude. I've done this for so many years that it's actually fun for me to pray about what discourages me.

So instead of dwelling on discouragement, invite God into the process: pray for the object of your discouragement.

Change from a "Me" Focus to a "God" Focus

This is a biggie. Most of my discouragement is about me. It's about my unrealized dreams and expectations. It happens when my needs are not getting met. I'm not getting my way. Someone is hurting me. That opportunity should have been mine, not his. Do you hear any common words? *Me. Mine. My.* And everyone knows that being self-focused causes *my*opia.

To limit discouragement we must move from a perspective that says, "It's all about me" to one that realizes, "It's all about God." Hebrews 12:2 says, "Let us fix our eyes on Jesus." When we fix our eyes on Him, it causes us to think about the bigger picture—it's living life with eternity on the radar. In the end God always wins. And we're on His team. That's the perspective! When we're thinking eternally, the stuff that discourages us seems so insignificant. Let me give you an example . . .

A couple years ago, I played on a church softball team that ended up winning the league championship. But in the final game—the biggest game of the season—I struck out. Struck out! In softball! I've played against senior citizens and legally blind people who didn't strike out. (There's an unwritten rule that men should never strike out in slow-pitch softball.)

Do you think I was discouraged? Absolutely! But we won the game and the championship! The discouragement of striking out was nothing compared to the joy of winning the championship. I got my three-inch-high plastic trophy and was voted MVP—Most Vanilla-like Player. It was awesome.

You're going to get discouraged in life. It happens. But if you're on God's team, the final game has already been won. You're part of the championship team. And life gets a lot better when you learn to live it in light of the ultimate celebration.

In light of eternity, the clutter is meaningless.

In light of eternity, the arguments in the backseat are noises of opportunity.

In light of eternity, the people I let down or who let me down . . . those are just windows for God's grace to shine. In light of eternity I'm a child of the Creator of the universe. He knitted me in my mother's womb (Psalm 139:13), and He knows my name and totally loves me. When our focus becomes eternal, discouragement can become the seedbed for a harvest of spiritual renewal—and the launchpad for a fresh start!

CHAPTER 8

BETTER TOGETHER

There's a phrase we use around our church a lot that I've really fallen in love with: "We are *better together*." I wish I could take credit for this saying, but I never come up with catchy phrases such as:

Revealing the feeling is the beginning of healing.

Self-worth and net worth are not the same.

Ask not what your country can do for you—ask what you can do for your country.

Me? My mind doesn't crank out many clever and memorable slogans.

They always come out sounding lame. Here are a few of my best efforts . . .

Give God your troubles, and He'll pop them like bubbles.

A verse a day keeps the demons away.

Nothing makes God laugh more than our plans—except SpongeBob. He cracks God up.

See what I mean? I will never write greeting cards or be known as a wordsmith.

But *better together* is a fantastic slogan. It simply means that when other people are in our lives, we'll thrive. It's a great idea . . . and it's biblical: "Two are better than one, because they have a good return for their work: If one falls down, his friend can help him up. But pity the man who falls and has no one to help him up!" (Eccl. 4:9–10).

Better together also means that God has created and called us into relationships. Not only has He summoned us into a personal relationship with Himself, but He invites us to have significant relationships with other humans. Apart from entering into those kinds of deep, real relationships, we cannot live the lives of abundance that God intended. But when we do have real, connecting relationships in our lives, we can:

know and be known;
love and be loved;
celebrate and be celebrated; and
serve and be served . . .

that's God's invitation to us today. Isn't that what you really want? It's part of the fresh-start package.

But here's the problem: the idea of *better together* can feel counter-cultural to how we're taught to live in America. We're the land of the free, the home of the brave, and mistakenly we translate that to mean we should do everything on our own. Here in Orange County we've even named our main airport after the movie star who exemplified rugged individualism, John Wayne. Did you ever see a John Wayne movie where his character needed anyone other than himself? Do you think John Wayne ever said, "Hey buddy, can we get together sometime for a Venti nonfat soy mocha and chat—I've got some things that are heavy on my heart"? Never! When it came to John Wayne, it was just him, his eye patch, and his horse. These days, you don't even see his horse. His statue at the airport stands all alone. No horse. No buddies. Not even any luggage.

Sometimes we're tempted to live our lives like John Wayne characters—capable and strong, perhaps, but alone and friendless too. Let's face it, friendships aren't always smooth. When they become difficult, there's always the temptation to quit. Friendships take real work. Sometimes they hurt. Or perhaps the bulk of our friendships are superficial. We know "of" people and they know "of" us, but that's about as far as things go. We go to church or our jobs and for years we sit in the same seat, smile at the same faces, chat with the same people about sports or weather or jobs or vacations or movies or even about God . . . but nobody really knows us. And we don't really know anybody else. We've convinced ourselves that we're fine or that we even prefer it that way, but deep down we know that's a lie. We've bought into the notion that we can do life on our own, but in our most honest moments we know we can't, and we don't want to.

So what do we do? Internally, we know we're lonely. We've hidden our real selves and the hurts inside—and we won't let anyone in. Nobody understands our secret aches and longings and hopes and dreams and fears. The people in our lives are just familiar strangers all the way to the grave. In fact, if we had a birthday party, what *really* close friends would be there?

And so, we're stuck. So how do we move beyond this loneliness that we won't admit? How do we get a fresh start in the area of deep friendships?

The Problem with Hiding

Recently I was speaking at a high school conference about this very topic of friendship, when I was approached by a man who was a chaperone from a visiting youth group. He said, "I'm fifty-three years old. I've grown up in church. My dad was a pastor, and I've got to tell you that I've never heard a sermon about genuine friendship. I must admit that I have no clue as to how to make a real friend."

It was a powerful and sad statement—one that characterizes many. You and I are wired to be connected to other humans. God created us to live within the context of others. Life works best when you and I have friends—I'm not referring to mere acquaintances; I'm talking about people who know you deeply and still love you. You and I cannot face life alone. We were designed to go through this journey rubbing shoulders with one another.

Here's how this unpacks: without a genuine commitment to live with a "better together" mentality, our default mode is to hide our real selves. Okay, but why is that a problem? We've already mentioned these next verses in this book, but they're so foundational to living life to the fullest that I want to look at them again: In Matthew 22:37–39, Jesus is talking about what's truly important in life. He says, "'Love the Lord your God with all your heart and with all your soul and with all your mind.' This is the first and greatest commandment. And the second is like it: 'Love your neighbor as yourself.'"

Loving others . . . that's the key. Whenever Jesus summarized God's will for people, He always did it in terms of relationship. We are created in the image of a relational God. He knows that for us to function properly, we must leave isolation and move into communities of friendship.

Think of it this way. If we live in isolation, we become . . .

» . . . like the young mom who gets angry at her small children and screams when no one is around. This is her secret, but she doesn't really want it to be. She wants to know if anybody out there is like her. She's hurting and feeling guilty—but she's all alone.

» . . . like the married couple who is known by everybody in their social circle for living the good life. Yet they're sleeping in separate bedrooms, and they never talk intimately between themselves. They look like the model couple, but they're hiding the painful reality of a crumbling marriage because they are too afraid to let anyone know they are not perfect.

» . . . like the college student who has been the pride of his mom and dad. He's been on the honor roll since kindergarten. But no one knows he's been cheating since junior high. He doesn't tell anybody, and the guilt is eating him alive.

» . . . like the man who keeps promising himself he won't go to that porn site *ever again* . . . but he does, over and over. He's caught in a cycle of failure and shame, which only leads him to fail all over again. And he has no one safe to tell.

Nobody knows their secrets, and they're so isolated. On and on it goes. How about you? What's your "secret" story? Who knows it? If you're not known intimately by a few good friends, if you don't have a desire to be "better together," you're not living as abundantly as you could . . . in essence, you're hiding. And when you're hiding, you're stuck.

I remember the first time I really realized I didn't want to do life on my own. I was in junior high and wanted to see the movie *Jaws* with a friend from the neighborhood. For reasons unknown to me, my parents actually said yes. That one decision resulted in many years of therapy. If you've never seen the movie, it's a virtual bloodbath of deep water, fish, gore, and an unforgettable sound track ("Da-dum . . . da-dum . . .").

Right in the opening credits, people get eaten; then the carnage goes from bad to worse. The movie ends with a guy being severed limb by bloody limb. It's not the type of scene you see on the fishing channel— pretty scary stuff.

I watched most of *Jaws* feeling like I was sitting on fishhooks. The closing credits brought no comfort for me. After the lights came on, the terror lingered. Even the water at the movie's drinking fountain was scary. Then I had to walk outside—what if Jaws was lurking in the parking lot? During our drive home, my friend and I were too frightened to speak. I lived at the end of a cul-de-sac, and once we reached our neighborhood, my ride dropped me off at his house—which was at the head of the street (because he didn't want to drive home alone). I begged him to take me home, since he was in a car and could race back to his house and pull into his garage to be safe, but he refused (too scared). I had to walk home past *five* houses. Actually, I ran home, I was still so scared of what might be out there in the dark.

Sprinting in the ink-black night along the front of people's lawns, I accidentally tripped over a sprinkler head. I couldn't see the obstacle, and my brain struggled to comprehend what had happened. I thought a shark reached out and caught my leg! As I fell headlong into the darkness, I was sure Jaws was preparing for a delicious Doug dinner.

Why do I share this embarrassing moment with you? Because any sort of terror brings to light the necessity of close friends. One day you'll face a crisis—not a fictional, amphibious one, but a real crisis. Maybe it will be the loss of a job, or problems with money, or someone you love getting seriously sick. You'll feel like Jaws has swum up underneath you. At that moment you will not want to be alone.

A few years ago I faced a real crisis when my father died. That was real, and it was a hurt like I had never known. My dad wasn't that old, and I wasn't really prepared for his death. Someone whom I loved and looked up to suddenly was no more. For months, I was in bad shape. Fortunately there were friends who upheld me through that dark season.

Unlike my childhood trip on the sidewalk, this time, I wasn't alone in my pain.

Deep friendships are more than a convenient way to manage crisis. Sure, it's great to have friends help us in dark seasons, but our need for friendships goes deeper than support. Close relationships are at the root of what life was meant to be about. Just before Christ went to the cross, He could have done anything, but He chose to spend time with His closest friends. Scripture preserves for us those friendship vignettes: the Last Supper; praying with Peter, James, and John in the garden; and even on the cross when He thought of His mother's well-being and asked John to look after her. Taking the sins of the world was something Christ did by Himself—in that moment He was separate from everything—but He walked through as much of the experience as possible with the help of His community of intimate and most cherished friends. His pattern of relationships shows us the way to live.

The Invitation to Friendship

I invite you to evaluate your friendships and push beyond the superficial. Move out of not being known to a place where you are known. Learn to develop the types of friends who can bring out the best in you and help you discover the greatness for which God designed you.

I have no doubt that real friendships are gifts of God. Friends are brought into our lives through prayer and God's blessing. He moves us close to other people, or them to us, because He wants to shape and mold us (and for us to shape and mold others). It's part of His sanctification design. God does the real work, of course, but often, He does it through people.

Now, we've all lived long enough to know that not all relationships will go to the deepest depths of friendship, but we can increase the quality of most friendships. Even so, not everyone will be our "best friend." Jesus Himself was always surrounded by people but had few very close friends. Many people knew Him and called Him "friend," but only a small number knew Him intimately. His other friends were on different levels of familiarity with Him.

Right now, let's look at three different relationships Jesus had. In doing so, we will see three different levels of friendship. These levels are my descriptions of various depths that I see in Scripture and ones I've personally experienced.

Walk with me down this path.

Connections

In Luke 19:1–10, Jesus connects briefly with someone He apparently doesn't know very well, a man named Zacchaeus. Not much is known about Zacchaeus, other than he was a short, influential man (imagine Danny DeVito in a robe). Zacchaeus learns that Jesus is coming his way, so to get above the crowds, he climbs up a sycamore tree for an unobstructed view. As Jesus comes by, He calls Zacchaeus by name and invites Himself to his home for dinner. It was a quick yet powerful connection—and the beginning of a friendship.

Every moment can open the door to this level of friendship. It begins simply by recognizing someone. It's not hard at all. A connecting friendship requires you to be . . . well . . . breathing. If you're alive, you can do this. You take notice. It doesn't mean you need to walk up to complete strangers and start connecting, not if it feels too weird for you. Just start with the circles of people who are normally around you—coworkers, neighbors, people at church, folks you see on a regular basis and perhaps have never spoken to. You recognize a person or something about that person and comment on it. It communicates that you care. What might you notice? Things like these:

> » *I've seen that guy with his son at my kids' soccer field.*
> » *My coworker has a Yankees bumper sticker on his car. I like the Yankees too.*
> » *Hey, new neighbors just moved in.*

» *This is the same cashier I had last week.*
» *What do you know—the guy in the pew in front of me is wearing the same shoes as me.*

Once you recognize and comment on something, the ice has been broken and you can either step in or dive in depending on your comfort level. It doesn't need to be anything bold. It could be as simple as more conversation. Notice that Jesus didn't just say, "Hey look up in that tree, it's Zacchaeus . . . a wee little man. Let's keep walking, disciples." No, He reached out to him. He extended an invitation for something more—a meal. Notice: He invited *Himself* to Zacchaeus's house. That's creative!

When I first began working at Saddleback Church, I hardly knew anyone. During our first year here, only three people extended an invitation to me to do something social. To be honest, it felt very lonely that first year. Now, years later, I simply can't accept all the invitations we get, and often I have to say no to others' attempts to reach out. But here's the point: if you're in a place of loneliness, you don't need to wait for others to extend invitations to you. Take the initiative and reach out. You may get rejected, but don't give up—try again. Sometimes we hit people at the wrong time, but we can't be defeated by their responses.

All relationships at the connecting level require some sort of risk. Many people are a lot like Zacchaeus . . . waiting for someone to take a risk and connect with them. They go through life alone, climbing trees and living by themselves and wondering what it would be like to journey with another—to be known, loved, and cared for.

Take the first step. Reach out. Risk. Invite someone out to coffee, or to your house. Maybe you think you could never do that. Your house is too small, or it's not clean enough, or you don't cook well, or your plates don't match the curtains. Who cares? Honestly, I've been to hundreds of people's houses, and I don't remember anything about the decor or meals. What I remember are the people who risked reaching out to pursue friendship.

Please know that I fully understand how scary this action can be. Last week, a family moved into our neighborhood, and we made cookies and took them to their house. Was that weird? Yes, a bit. It sort of felt like we were announcing, "Hi, neighbors! We're the Cleaver family!" But it all worked out well in the end. The family didn't open the door and say, "Whoa, you look more like the Munsters." This time the connection was successful.

Recognize, reach out, risk—those are the first steps in the connecting level of friendships.

Friends-in-Process

Cultivate. This is a word we aren't too familiar with these days, unless we're into gardening or farming, but it's a great concept as it relates to your *friends-in-process*. It communicates movement. Think turning a shovelful of dirt upside down.

Now, my method of gardening, or landscaping, or doing anything with soil usually involves saying, "Uh . . . who do I write this check to?" But friendship gardening is a do-it-yourself project. The Bible records a relationship between Jesus and Peter that was constantly being cultivated. Even if we don't know much about cultivating, we can learn from this example.

Peter was an amazingly inconsistent guy. He was headstrong, passionate, and impulsive. One minute he was declaring his unswerving allegiance to Christ; the next minute he was denying Him. At one point, Jesus addressed Peter by saying, "Get behind me, Satan!" (Matt. 16:23)—how's that for a rocky friendship?!

Yet in spite of the tension that sometimes existed between Peter and Jesus, Peter was considered one of the top three closest to Christ. Though there were twelve disciples, we nearly always read about Peter, James, and John. During the most difficult times in His life, Jesus had His go-to friends. Peter was one of them.

How does this apply to us? Let's make this personal. Who are three friends with whom you have experienced both the highs and lows? The good times and the tough ones? Let me offer some ways you may be able to cultivate these types of friendships.

Encourage. Here's the truth about encouragement: people are dying for it! Everyone needs it! Encouragement is one of the most powerful ways to breathe life into a relationship. People can never get too much of it—I've never heard someone say, "Stop encouraging me—I've had it up to here with all your kind comments."

We often try to reason our way out of encouraging someone, using excuses like these:

» "She already knows it."
» "If I tell him, he'll just get a big head."
» "People must say nice things to her all the time."

But the core principle of encouragement is this: if you think something nice about a person . . . go ahead and say it.

The best kinds of encouragement focus on things that really matter—not externals. It's not about telling someone that you like his car, or her clothes or hair; it's commenting on character, kindness, Christlikeness. It's saying things like these:

» "I love the way you treat your child."
» "You're a great small group leader."
» "I appreciate how you ask questions whenever we talk. I feel like you really care about me."

When a friend breathes life into another friend by means of encouragement, it helps make the other person become more alive. It adds value to him and may even motivate him toward a fresh start.

Some are so good at this! They breathe life into people so naturally. They see a big "10" on other people's foreheads, and they treat them like that. They live the words of Hebrews 10:24: "Think of ways to encourage one another to outbursts of love and good deeds" (NLT).

Think of the most encouraging person in your life. Maybe it is a parent, a coach, or your spouse. This person really believes in you. He or she sees great potential in you and encourages you regularly to live up to all you can be. For me, it was my dad. He constantly warmed my soul by telling me these simple words: "I believe in you." Who do you know who could stand to hear those words today?

Encouragement can be a lot of fun. I have a friend at church in her late seventies, and I whistle every time I see her. She wrote me a note that said, "You never get too old to appreciate it when someone whistles at you." I love it!

Confront. How many times have you held back the truth that someone needed to hear because you were afraid? Maybe you wanted to be liked. Or you didn't want to create conflict. Perhaps you wanted another date. Or to keep your job.

But with deeper friendships, sometimes a loving confrontation is needed. Healthy confrontation isn't bad for us. At its best, it's iron sharpening iron (Prov. 27:17). The Bible also says in that same chapter, "Wounds from a friend are better than many kisses from an enemy" (v. 6 NLT).

At this friend-in-process level of friendship, I would actually encourage you to invite healthy confrontation into your life. Real friends help grow and develop their friends. They influence one another to become better parents, spouses, and friends. If we fail to confront when needed, we tend to hold grudges against the person for not changing, and that's neither fair for your friend nor good for you.

Real confrontation is never meant to tear someone down. It's always done to build someone up. When we invite this type of confrontation into a friendship, we're saying to the other person, "Please don't allow me to get away with things that might be hurtful to others."

How do you lovingly confront a friend who needs to be challenged?

There's no one way, but here are some different approaches to starting the conversation. Begin with things like:

- » "I care about our relationship too much to not mention this . . . "
- » "I need to talk to you about some of your actions that I think are going to harm you . . . "
- » "I feel this way when you . . . "

Truth can sting, but if it's said with the right motive, then it's really a gift. When we hold back truth, we hold back love.

Of course, equal parts of love and truth are difficult to give, and it's okay to be careful in this area. If the truth you speak into others' lives isn't spoken in the context of love, or if it isn't prayerfully considered and it represents your own ego (or your own hurt), then it doesn't do anything for a person.

Anyone can be critical. Believe me; I've got stacks of letters proving this point. But real confrontation is done not with a spirit of criticism but always with the motivation of building the other person up. And who knows? Your willingness to confront might be the catalyst to someone else's fresh start!

Commit Time. Relationships on a deeper level require a lot of shared experiences. They don't have to take years to build, but they do need intentional, regular time.

For instance, one of my friends, who was very close to me during the time of my dad's death, is someone I've logged a lot of hours with. This guy went to the mortuary and helped me choose from more than 100 different casket choices. He walked the cemetery yard and helped me find a plot. He helped me clean out my dad's stuff. He comforted me when I cried. He was there to listen. Over fifteen years of friendship, we've done a lot together: golfed, camped, vacationed, "Jacuzzied," shared holidays, and traveled—together. We weren't always intentional about encouraging and confronting each other at these times, but just being together created an environment for a deeper relationship to happen.

It can't be forced. And a deep friendship can't be arranged like a Far Eastern marriage. There are no shortcuts. There is no spiritual drive-thru where you can say, "I'll take one cherished friend, please—and supersize him." Close, intimate friendships must be cultivated by spending quality time together.

Lead with Listening. Here's a basic relationship rule I try to follow: No one is interested in connecting with a world-class talker. People want to be heard. When you know a person is a good listener, you can't wait to connect with him or her. So, for a relationship to last, active listening is essential.

James 1:19 says, "Post this at all the intersections, dear friends: Lead with your ears, follow up with your tongue, and let anger straggle along in the rear" (MSG). This is fundamental wisdom that is vital to quality relationships. Listen. Just listen. Ask open-ended questions of the other person, and get him talking. Then listen. When you follow this pattern of interaction, it communicates a very powerful message to whomever you're with. It says, "You're important to me. You have something worth saying. And I want to hear it."

Now, what about that third type of friendship? Who are the people at the deepest level of relationship with us, who know us best and love us most?

Cherished Friends

There's something inside the human heart that cries to be seen, known, and *loved*. At this third level of friendship, we don't hide anything from the other person. We are emotionally transparent with each other as we journey together. This is the epitome of "better together." A good example of this is the relationship between Jesus and John, the disciple often referred to as the one whom Jesus loved.

In John 13:23, at the Last Supper, John leans against the chest of Jesus as they are eating dinner. In Jewish culture, it was common to recline around low tables. Leaning toward one another was not unusual—among people who were close. It expressed deep friendship. Later, when Jesus went to the cross, it was this same John who stood at the foot of the cross, comforting Jesus' mother, Mary. Where were the rest of the disciples? Judas had just been out collecting money to betray Him. Peter was swearing he didn't know Him. Most of the other disciples were hiding in fear for their lives. But it was John, whom Jesus cherished, who was at His side till the end.

I believe this friendship level is characterized by at least three key components:

Trust. In John 19:26–27, Jesus told John to take care of His mother. That's a sign of trust, and trust is the foundation of this type of friendship. Trust is both an emotional and willful act. Emotionally, it is where you expose your vulnerabilities to a friend, believing that he or she will not take advantage of your openness but will instead behave in a caring and loving manner toward you. Willfully, then, you choose to share with him your secrets, hurts, and dreams.

Transparency. There is a deep connection between being transparent and being cherished. You can only fully cherish a person, or he can only cherish you, when there are no walls between you, and you know each other through and through. To have cherished friends, and friends who cherish you in return, you must continually work to know and be known. Cherishing a person requires complete familiarity and the removal of all facades. It requires an honesty that doesn't hide. And when your real self is known, a friend at this level meets you with a smile of acceptance. He sees you, and you see him, warts and all. You know that he is not perfect, yet you love the person regardless. And the feeling is mutual.

Beauty. I realize that "beauty" isn't a male-friendly word (sorry, guys), but there's something beautiful about the depth of friendship where you can be together and feel safe, known, and loved for who you are.

At this level of relationship:

» you don't feel pressure to hide;
» you don't have to always talk (there can be comfortable silence in the air); and
» you are who you truly are.

What a great thing that is! I don't know any other word to better describe this level of friendship than *beauty*.

Along the Road of True Friendship

When I think of friendship, three images come to mind.

Friendship is sometimes like a lump of unformed clay. It just sits there like a big, gray blob of muck. It's undeveloped; it's not good for much . . . but it has potential. It's just going to take some work to shape it.

Friendship is sometimes like a lump of clay that's being formed. Time and intention have been put into it. Maybe it's developing the shape of a bowl or an urn or a mug. The friendship is nice, it could be functional, but it isn't yet all it's meant to be.

But friendship is occasionally like a beautiful vase. Here, the clay that started as a lump has been formed and put through the fire. When it comes out the other side, it's complete. It's functional, and it's all it's meant to be. It's a thing of beauty.

That's always God's invitation with friendships: to let them be all they can be.

These types of friendships are always within our grasp. God brings them our way, and He invites our cooperation in their forming. If you've been holding back, drowning in a pool of isolation, the good news is that you can get a fresh start today! Don't wait. Find someone. Connect. Cultivate. And commit to cherish your newfound friendship. Seize the day! Because, remember, we're always *better together*.

CHAPTER 9

REDEEMED REJECTION

Have you ever noticed how rejection is such a consistent part of life?

Having been a youth pastor for more than two decades, I know a lot about this. Rejection and youth ministry are synonymous. Teenagers can be incredibly blunt. Many don't fully realize that adults have feelings. They tell you exactly what they think, and often don't pull any punches when it comes to tact. For years I regularly heard statements like these:

- » "My mom said she likes your new haircut. But I think it looks stupid."
- » "I brought my friend to hear you speak last week. You weren't very good."

» "I used to think you were kind of an attractive sort of dad-type . . . until last week's waterslide trip, when I saw you in your bathing suit."

And so it went.

Apart from my experiences working with teenagers, I've battled for years with feelings of low self-worth and the fear of rejection. I think a lot of us do, whether we admit it or not. Battling rejection is a constant struggle in life.

Rejection can appear in many forms. Seldom as adults do we actually experience overt types of rejection, like: "Hey, Doug, I wanted to make an appointment so we could get together and I could reject you." If only rejection were that obvious, it would be a lot easier to either avoid or deal with. But it's usually a lot more subtle. We are born and raised and we go to school and get married and get jobs and start families and live life and grow old in cultures that choose favorites and reject seconds. And since nobody can be the best at everything, all of us at one point or another have been ignored, overlooked, shunned, talked down to, bad-mouthed, insulted, discarded, picked last, and rejected by parents, teachers, friends, coaches, spouses, our own kids, and more.

Maybe right now you're feeling rejected. You put your time, talent, or treasure forward, and it wasn't received the way you had hoped. Now you want to pick up the pieces and go forward in your spiritual journey with God, but something's holding you back. Maybe you're angry at the person who rejected you—and fearful that someone else will do it again. Maybe you're annoyed that your efforts or giftings weren't received like they should have been (what if they aren't next time either?). Maybe you're simply sad—sad for the way things could have been. If only you hadn't been rejected . . .

It's Part of Life

Some of you are having a hard time admitting that you have even experienced rejection. You're denying it. You're strong, self-sufficient types, the kind of people who shed water off your backs like ducks in a pond. Criticism doesn't bother you—you don't even notice it.

Or do you?

Take a few moments to think back through your life. As you're thinking, let me give you some prompters. Have you ever experienced any of the following?

» **Professional rejection.** You didn't get a job. Someone got the contract instead of you. You weren't given a much-deserved raise. You were overlooked for a promotion. Your company downsized and said you're no longer needed. You gave years of your life to a profession and weren't thanked or compensated or even patted on the back for a job well done.

» **Physical rejection.** You weren't good-looking enough. Somebody said (or inferred) that your nose isn't right; you are too short or too tall; your hairline is receding (that's me); you have chicken legs (yep, me again); you're overweight (that's becoming me)—and that person chose someone else.

» **Parental rejection.** You did something, and your parents didn't approve. Maybe this happened when you were a child—you put forth your best effort, and it was met by a grunt from your father or a shrug from your mother. Or maybe this happened when you were an adult—you still long for your parents' approval, but it's not there.

» **Rejection from your kids.** Parents of teenagers experience this on a regular basis. They regularly hear things like: *You're too old. You don't get it. You don't understand. You're not fair.*

Parents of toddlers experience this too. They hear things like: *No. No-no-no! My way. I hate you!* Your parenting skills and efforts are vastly underappreciated. Few people know this, but I'm sure that little children secretly meet in those McDonald's jungle gyms and share tips with each other on how to reject their parents.

» **Recreational rejection.** One of the most brutal practices in the history of childhood is where peers line up and pick teams. You're standing there praying your guts out that you won't be picked last. Have you ever heard the dreaded "Okay, I *guess* we'll take you . . ."?

» **Academic rejection.** You got a lousy grade on something, even though you did your best. You failed a class. A teacher implied that you were slow, or stupid, or weren't trying your hardest, or would never amount to much.

» **Dating rejection.** You want to date somebody, but that person doesn't feel the same way about you. Or you aren't asked out—ever. Or you're in a relationship and then get dumped. Or a person doesn't respond to your advances. Or you ask someone out and the person says no because she's washing her hair—every night for the next two years.

» **Marital rejection.** Marital rejection can happen so many ways. You want to talk, but your husband would rather watch football. Or you want sex, but your wife would rather talk. Or, worst of all, you want to stay married, but your spouse doesn't.

» **Spiritual rejection.** Sad to say, but this type of rejection is typically felt as a result of the actions of a church community. You do or say something, and the group disapproves. Or they all act one way, and you don't go along, and so you're criticized or ignored for it. You try to get involved in the church, but you can't. You feel like an outcast. They're insiders; you're not.

Some of the rejection we experience is intentional—people choose to hurt us. But much of it is accidental—either people are insensitive or clueless, or they think they're talking behind our backs but we're really nearby and hear it anyway. It all adds up over the years. So what's the result?

When we experience consistent rejection, here are some of the things we tend to do:

» We become emotionally insecure. We start to wonder if our feelings are valid. We are unsure of what to think or feel. We don't speak the truth because we never want to disappoint anyone.

» We become approval addicts who go beyond the call of duty to please others—even if it's painful to us or our families.

» We live in fear of rejection. We don't want to voice our opinions too loudly, lest someone object. We stifle our creativity: if we put too much of ourselves into a project, someone is bound to criticize it—and that would tear us apart.

» We become afraid of others. People have hurt us, so we decide that we will do whatever it takes to avoid being hurt: we avoid people.

» We disguise pain with performance. We are afraid of being critiqued, so we try harder at whatever we do. We mistakenly think that if we're perfect, we won't be rejected.

One of the saddest things about living with rejection is that often we develop a skewed understanding about God. We start to think that He's always sitting on our shoulders, ready and eager to bust our chops for any infraction of the rules. We forget that He loves us, and that His love is abundant and complete.

For instance, I grew up in a situation where I believed that the mark of a Christian was a complicated list of don'ts. If you *don't* smoke, drink, chew, swear, dance, go to the theater, and play cards—then you're a good Christian.

But one day, when I was about sixteen, I watched my dog Rudy walk by. Rudy was a collie and a marvelous dog. Then it hit me—Rudy didn't smoke, drink, chew, swear, dance, go to the theater, or play cards. If avoiding those things was what a Christian was all about, then Rudy was a better Christian than I was. I felt like a reject.

It is not the purpose of this book to argue over what is or isn't acceptable for a follower of Christ. I'm telling you that God isn't about rejection, regardless of your performance or lack of it. He loves the whole world—that's why He sent His only Son, Jesus. *Whoever* believes in Jesus will have eternal life (John 3:16). He doesn't care if you have a big nose or can't play baseball or failed your geometry test or want to talk more than your husband wants to listen. His arms are always open wide.

And one of the amazing things about Jesus is that He understands what it feels like to be rejected. Though He was perfect, He was still despised and rejected (Isa. 53:3). If you've been rejected, know that you're in good company. You're not alone. Jesus knows exactly what you're going through.

But how does knowing that help you? It's *you* who have been rejected this time. You need a fresh start, but how do you move beyond the memories of all those past rejections?

Abundant Action Plans

God is more than able to remove the effects of rejection from our lives. But for Him to do that, *we* must be willing to trade in the lies we have bought into in exchange for His truth. We have to get a *new perspective*—of Him, of ourselves, and of those who have rejected us. Let's start with them.

Realize That People Will Inevitably Let You Down

Yes, people will let you down. It's a simple fact, but somehow knowing it and articulating it helps us move past the pain of rejection. Humans can never satisfy all our needs. We long to be fully loved, and we are hurt when people can't satisfy the longings that only God can satisfy. When we look to others for the ultimate answers, we are inevitably going to feel disappointed—and rejected.

What's worse, we place far too much value on people's opinions. We're shaped by their words and tyrannized by what they may think of us. God knows this, so He tries to teach us to put people in their proper perspective. Consider Isaiah 51:12: "I . . . am the one who comforts you. So why are you afraid of mere humans, who wither like the grass and disappear?" (NLT).

Don't be surprised when someone rejects you or hurts you in any way. There is sin in the world. It does exist. People can be angry and evil. Hurt people will lash out at others. Rejected people will reject others. This shouldn't surprise anyone. Jeremiah 17:9 says, "The human heart is most deceitful and desperately wicked. Who really knows how bad it is?" (NLT).

Let's say someone reads this book and writes me a letter that says, "Doug Fields: You are the worst author in the world. Your books are horrible. Your writing is horrible. Your content is horrible. Your jokes are worse than horrible. In fact, you're horrible—you should get thrown out of a plane." I might be wounded briefly, but I wouldn't quit doing what I do, and I wouldn't think that I'm no longer worthy to be a messenger of God. If I met my critic face to face, I might encourage him to try reading the works of other authors—some dead ones perhaps. (Death might resonate well with his ultra-encouraging spirit.) But I wouldn't be shaken at my core. Why? Because I have the right *perspective*. My ultimate worth is not derived from other people's opinions of me (especially strangers). People are designed to let me down, to hurt me, and to reject me. They rejected Christ. Why not reject me too? Or you?

One of the most helpful, practical things you can do is develop a plan ahead of time to help you deal with rejection. That's right—I'm suggesting you develop a rejection *plan*. Or call it a "Rational Response Plan" (RRP), if that sounds more helpful and official. But whatever its name, have a plan in place so you're not paralyzed and in turmoil the next time you face rejection and your feelings come gushing out.

Let's think about this for a few minutes. You already have a typical rejection response, right? When you're rejected, what's the default emotion that typically emerges in your life? Is it anger? Moodiness? Do you feel depressed? Do you want to just go eat a tub of ice cream?

My natural response to rejection is to feel defeated. When criticism comes my way, I think things like, "I'm a worm, a complete loser. My fourth-grade guidance counselor was right—I'll never amount to anything."

But here's my RRP. Actually, I have two of them. The first is for people I know and already have some kind of relationship with. The second is for anonymous critics. Let's look at my two RRPs, one by one.

RRP #1: Deal with it immediately. If I feel rejected by someone I know, my rational response plan is to confront the person as soon as possible. I don't want negative emotions to simmer and fester. I might mull it over for twenty-four hours while I pray about the situation or collect my thoughts, but never longer than that. My conscious decision is never to allow something to simmer and become ugly and give birth to bitterness.

So I go to the person I feel rejected by and ask a clarifying question. My questions usually start out something like one of these:

>> "I'm curious about what you meant when you said . . ."
>> "Hey, can we talk? I'm feeling a little stung."

Then, if the rejection is rooted in something valid, I'll listen to it. I'm not perfect, and maybe this person needs to tell me something about my personality or ministry that needs honing. Part of my RRP is a conscious effort to listen without getting defensive. If the criticism is valid, I need to know about it. Besides, what you *think* is rejection might be nothing more than well-intentioned correction. Don't confuse the two. If it is rejection, dealing with it immediately might just turn the situation around and give you a fresh start.

RRP #2: Ignore it completely. You'll notice that both my rational rejection plans are pretty simple: If I know the person and value the relationship, I deal with the conflict immediately. If I don't know the person, I ignore the criticism completely. It's that simple.

A few examples here: I have a neighbor who complained a while back that I had too many people over at my house one night and too many cars on the (public) street. She didn't even talk to me about it rationally; she just yelled at me. She made it clear that she doesn't want to be friends. But that's okay. I have no relationship with this woman. So when she yelled at me, I listened, smiled, then continued with life. It was an irrational moment based more on her loneliness or hurt or emptiness than on the cars on the street. Basically, I didn't allow her anger to stick. Life is too short to get upset every time I see this neighbor. Whenever I see her now, I just wave (which I think makes her mad).

Another example: A few years after coming on staff at Saddleback, I went to my pastor Rick Warren and asked him how he handled the anonymous letters of criticism from our congregation. I got plenty— letters from people in the church who had an opinion about what I wore, said, thought, did, ate . . . nothing was off-limits. Some of them clearly read like personal rejection. It was unbelievable! Each note was anonymous, so there was no way to hear the person's heart or dialogue with him or her. I figured that if the people writing the notes truly cared about bettering something, they would have had the courage to sign them. These were all about rejection.

I said, "Rick, do you ever get these?"

He started chuckling! "Of course," he answered. "I get plenty."

"So, what do you do about it?" I asked.

Then came one of the best pieces of rejection advice I've ever received. Rick said simply, "I don't read them."

What? Wow! I never imagined that was even an option. Rick had his RRP already in place—any critical card or letter that came in without a name was thrown away. In fact, it was tossed by his assistant before it ever got to him.

I've adopted that same plan for the last several years. In a congregation of twenty thousand people, I get five to ten anonymous critique cards after every sermon I preach. That might not sound like much, but if you multiply that by twenty years or so . . . that's a lot of rejection that I don't need to experience anymore because they are thrown out before I ever see them.

The point of developing an RRP is to be proactive when it comes to rejection. You know how to deal with rejection before it arrives. Your RRP will undoubtedly look different from mine, depending on the specifics of your life. For instance, perhaps you're single, and you need to develop an RRP designed for the dating world. Maybe you ask somebody out and the person says no—what do you do? With an RRP already in place, it takes the guesswork out of your response. Maybe your RRP is to smile, give a gracious response, realize that there's someone for everyone—then run three miles that night after work. Whatever is a positive outlet for you.

Or maybe you're a mother whose constant source of rejection is your junior-high boy—who suddenly doesn't want your hugs anymore and withers in embarrassment when he has to be seen in public with you. You're old. You're clueless. You're so behind the times—or so he tells you. And heaven forbid if you touch him—especially in front of his friends! So maybe the best RRP for you is to shrug, realize it's just a stage he's going through (this, too, shall pass), then mentally look forward to the day he complains to you about *his* touch-me-not teen.

How do you develop your RRP? The answer becomes easier when you answer a more foundational question: Who am I going to live my life for—God or humans?

If the answer is humans—it's a setup for rejection. Why? Because you can't please everybody. You get one group pleased and the other group gets pi—uh . . . mad. Anyone who has multiple children knows this scenario: If you ask, "Where do you want to eat tonight?" one kid says, "Arby's," and the other kid says, "Yuck!" The second kid says, "Taco Bell," and the first kid feigns vomiting. (Incidentally, my specific RRP for this scenario involves me saying, "I'll settle this. We're going to eat free samples at Costco.")

Even God can't please everybody. One person wants it to rain, and another person wants the sun out. One person wants the Celtics to win the big game; the other prays for the Lakers. The secret of simplifying life is saying, "I'm going to do what pleases God. If I live to please God, it's always the right thing to do. It doesn't matter what anybody else thinks." In Galatians 1:10, Paul put this in black and white: "I'm not trying to be a people pleaser! No, I am trying to please God. If I were still trying to please people, I would not be Christ's servant" (NLT).

You and I have a choice. We can choose whether we're going to live for the applause of God or the applause of people. The crowd or God? This Scripture says we can't seek the approval of both at the same time.

Focus on How God Views You

God sees you differently than people do. People look at externals; God looks at the heart. Consider 1 Samuel 16:7: "The LORD doesn't make decisions the way you do! People judge by outward appearance, but the LORD looks at a person's thoughts and intentions" (NLT).

The context of this verse is that God had ordered the prophet

Samuel to appoint the new king of Israel. Samuel was told to find this new king at the house of Jesse. When he got there, Jesse paraded out seven of his sons. When Samuel saw the first, he immediately thought his job was over. The first son was the tallest, strongest, and most handsome of Jesse's boys. Samuel thought, *This must surely be the next king of Israel.* But God had a different plan in mind. God's choice for king was the youngest son, a ruddy shepherd boy, fresh from the fields, who was barely old enough to wipe his own nose. His name was David, and he would become one of the most powerful and God-fearing kings the nation of Israel would ever have.

God always sees our potential. He knows who we are and who we can be. While other people look at the externals of our lives—our cars, homes, degrees, bank accounts, clothes—and accept or reject us accordingly, God sees the heart. He also sees us as His own children (1 John 3:2), wholly and dearly loved. That's the perspective we need: that we are God's *children*—and He never rejects His own.

Let's dwell on this point for a while—God's amazing love for us—because our understanding of this is key to moving beyond rejection. Having Someone great and awesome who loves and cares for you is quite powerful.

A few years back I was watching *Cinderella* with my daughter. I know it's just a cartoon, but it always upsets me the way Cinderella is treated. I don't like the wicked stepmother; I don't like the mean sisters. And it pains me that they reject Cinderella and view her as ugly and worthless and good-for-nothing.

A lot of people think the high point of the Cinderella story is when she goes to the ball wearing the glass slippers and all, but when the magic ends at midnight, it's important to note that Cinderella's life goes back to the way it's always been. The next day, her family would still abuse her. Her life only really changes at the very end—when the slipper fits and the prince loves her and they live happily ever after.

After watching the video with my little girl, I listened to my inner "pastor voice" telling me that this was a prime time to make theological applications about . . . uh, well . . . everything, so I began to tell her that the prince is to Cinderella sort of like who Jesus is to us. The prince saw in Cinderella something that other people didn't see. He placed value on someone who didn't feel loved. God is this way with us. But instead of a glass slipper, God puts a "grace" slipper on us—He gives us a love we don't deserve. He sees in us what other people don't see. He crowns us with value and potential. And He invites us away from being unwanted stepchildren to dance with Him and join His kingdom. I thought it was a great point and my connections of theology to cinema were outstanding—but she said, "Can we watch another cartoon instead of talking?"

Fully comprehending God's love for us gives us power over rejection. His love is unconditional. He knows everything about us—and still loves us. We can whip ourselves into a frenzy, trying to live for the empty, false, often temporary approval of others, or we can resign from that losing game and fall back into God's permanent, boundless love. This love has the power to stop our heads from moving side to side to see what other people think of us. This love focuses our eyes on the One whose opinion of us really matters—God. Ephesians 1:4 describes it this way: "Long ago, even before he made the world, God loved us and chose us in Christ to be holy and without fault in his eyes" (NLT).

Wow. *Without fault.* That's how God sees you. Nobody else sees you that way. When you stand before humans, they see your flaws: the thinning hair, the expanding waist, the string of failures. But God sees you as pure, perfect, worthy of a fresh start—and that's how you should see you too.

How does this apply to our dealing with rejection?

Well, if God likes me, then who cares what anybody else thinks? If God hasn't rejected me, then who is anyone else to? Because God loves me, I don't have to prove my self-worth. That is so relaxing. I don't need the props anymore to make me feel good about myself. I don't have to wear a certain kind of clothes or drive a certain kind of car or have certain status symbols around my house to make me feel not rejected. I don't need them. God has looked at me and said, "This guy is valuable." To think that God is deeply concerned about me as a particular person immediately gives great purpose and enormous meaning to my short sojourn on this planet. It also gives me the impetus I need to recover from the pain of rejection. It will do the same for you.

Now that you've got your perspectives straight—the right view of yourself, the One who loves you (God), and those who have rejected you—how do you go about the business of moving ahead after rejection? How can you make a fresh start?

Begin to Dispense Compassion

There is a powerful action that we can take whenever we've been rejected. We can only do this with God's power moving fiercely inside us, but we *can* do it. Once we realize His great love for us, and that we have nothing to gain by proving our worth to other people, we can move beyond our feelings and actions of self-justification and begin to see our accusers as Christ sees them: with compassion.

How do we do this? Well, when we feel rejected, we always have a choice. We can turn inward and call ourselves losers, or we can look outward and extend God's grace to the people (or institutions) who are the source of our hurt. Here are some practical examples of this:

» Have you been rejected by a parent? Then see this parent with compassion. Something hurtful must have happened to your parent to make him or her this way.

» Were you rejected for no good reason by an employer? A company built on unsound business practices won't last for very long. How sad for them. The company could have been great, if only they hadn't worked to destroy it. Don't wish the worst for them. Be sorry that, in time, the whole company may suffer if there's not an internal change of heart. Pray for the employees who remain.

» Are you being rejected by a spouse? This is so difficult, because chances are that you are in constant interaction with a person who doesn't treat you right. Pray that God will give you compassion for your spouse. Again, something hurtful must have happened in his or her life to make your spouse act this way. Make it your aim to overwhelm your spouse with God's love as it flows through you. Extend to him or her the compassion that Christ gives you.

» Have you been rejected by a church? Was that church full of uptight people who wanted you to act or dress or speak in a straight-laced way? Or maybe that church was full of undisciplined people who wanted you to let it all hang out in ways that made you uncomfortable. Whatever way it hurt, have compassion on that church, and pray for its leaders—it's missing some important truths about what Christ came to do. It's focused on externals, and Christ always focuses on the heart.

Let me give you a little illustration about compassion in action. It's a bit superficial, but it points to how our rejection can be redeemed. God can turn our rejection into goodness and use it for His glory. What's more, our rejection can make us incredibly empathetic with anybody facing similar difficult times.

I love to laugh. I love teaching with humor—my thought is that tough truth always goes down a lot easier when the congregation's mouths are open. When I was growing up, my mentor was a pastor who always wove a lot of jokes into his messages. I wanted to speak like that, but I couldn't do it. I was lousy at telling jokes. So about fifteen years ago, I took a stand-up comedy class. The class's format involved the students developing and practicing our routines for four weeks and then performing a fifteen-minute set at the Improv—a local comedy club full of real, live people who weren't our classmates.

I must admit, on the night of the big show . . . I completely bombed!

People started booing after my first few jokes. They totally rejected me. So, I stopped and started and stumbled through nearly my whole routine—everything I had so carefully crafted—and I still had ten minutes to go. Even people closest to me said things like, "Yeah, Doug, that was rough." It was one of the most humiliating times of my life.

But do you know what that experience did for me? It made me more compassionate. If you want to try anything risky in your life, invite me along—I'll be there to cheer you on! (And I promise not to boo.) I have a huge heart for anyone who does anything on stage in front of other people. I know how hard it can be. You can bet I won't reject you.

There's something that happens whenever you take that which has been rejected and broken in you and offer it to others in the form of compassion and understanding. This is the type of love that can change and help other people, and open their hearts to the ways of God.

Well on Your Way

Do you feel stuck because of the rejection in your life? There is hope. God can redeem the rejection for His glory. He can make all things new. He is willing and able to offer you a new start today on your spiritual journey.

Our part is to cooperate with His plan. We do that by knowing the truth of any situation—that people are fallen and will let us down. They don't have the perspective of us that God does.

So next, we focus on His love for us. The God of the universe calls us *beloved*. He is crazy about us. He's the only one whose opinion of us really matters.

Once we know and sense how deeply God adores and treasures us, we are that much more able to be compassionate toward the sources of our rejection. We can see them through God's eyes. The rejection loses its power over us. We can then be tools in God's hands to heal the pain of others' rejection. And isn't that what you want to be—someone God can use to heal others?

So come on! Embrace a fresh start. Live for an audience of One—and discover the abundant life that He promises.

CHAPTER 10

ANALYZED ANGER

Awhile ago I surveyed our church congregation and asked people to list the actions, behaviors, and attitudes of heart that they struggled with most. The item at the top of the list was not what I had initially imagined it would be—it *wasn't* compulsive spending or lust or pride or depression or workaholism or busyness or fear or anxiety or insecurity or family problems—or despair because their favorite sports' team didn't make the playoffs.

It was anger.

Though I was surprised at first, when I mulled over this response, it made sense—a lot of sense. As I work with people, even people who love and follow Jesus Christ, it seems as though I see traces of anger everywhere. I see it in the grocery store lineups, while waiting for a table at busy restaurants, and on the freeway on the way home from work. I see it in the faces and voices of parents at their kids' sporting events. I hear about it in our schools, particularly after a round of parent-teacher interviews or after a budget increase (or cut). I read it in e-mails and in postings on blogs. I observe it in relationships—how people talk about other people, the looks that come over their faces, the choices of words they use. Anger comes into my office and sits in my counseling chair. I see its aftermath in messed-up hearts, relationships, and lives.

This chapter *isn't* about what to do if you're a victim of anger; it's about what to do with the anger in your own life. If the former has been your experience, I want you to know that I am so sorry for your pain that someone's anger has caused you. The wounds of anger don't easily disappear. It takes a lot of courage to seek help and deal with the wounds you wear. It also takes a lot of courage to learn how to stop the pain cycle so you don't, in turn, damage others (make sure you read the chapter on forgiveness).

But let's focus on our own lives in this chapter. Let's focus on the anger that's closest to home, and own that which is ours. Sometimes we don't want to admit we're angry people. Maybe we're not. But chances are, if we peel back the outer layers, we'll see more anger in our lives than we care to admit. Sometimes anger is overt. At other times, it is much more subtle.

Personally, I've had a lot of experience with ungodly anger. I don't like what anger does to me. I don't like the confusing and out-of-control feelings it generates, and I don't like where my thoughts (and sometimes actions) end up when I'm angry. I know for a fact that my anger has wounded relationships. I'm sure I've chased people away from church because of an angry response to criticism. I have disappointed my friends. I have scared my children. I've hurt my wife with words fueled by anger. Sadly, I know anger well.

A while back I asked my family to make a list of times when they've unjustly been the recipients of my anger. Thankfully, it was a pretty short list . . . uh, about the same size as a phone book. I thought the list would actually be a lot bigger. Well, actually the phone book was just my wife's list. The kids' lists were so long, we had to go to Kinko's to get more paper.

Seriously, several years ago I became aware that often when I became angry, the way I handled my anger tended to cause fear in my children. I never thought I had a problem in this area because I wasn't violent (I'd just raise my voice); but sometimes it's hard to comprehend the power and influence we hold over people—particularly our own families. I wasn't aware that I was actually misappropriating my anger, so I never felt like I needed to worry about it. Then one day I got a wake-up call when my wife pulled me aside and said, "Hey, Dr. Jekyll, the kids get scared when you express anger like that." I was stunned, but I definitely listened. The next time I felt myself getting close to a flare-up, I paused long enough to glance at my children. Sure enough, they had already braced themselves for what they were sure was coming. I could see the truth of my wife's words in their eyes, and it broke my heart.

I know I'm not alone in the struggle to control and express anger. Plenty of people have no idea what to do when they're angry. Maybe this is you too. Chances are, anger was never modeled properly in your home when you were young, so you have no idea what to do with anger now that you're an adult. Or maybe you take your cues from what you see on TV and in the movies, where people regularly blow up at other people and storm out, and it tends to get results—but it never seems to work that way when you try it. Maybe you get violent. You're ashamed of it, but it's the truth. In anger, you terrorize the ones you love. On the other hand, maybe you believe anger is something you should never feel. Good Christians don't get angry—do they? So you stuff your anger deep down inside you and never let it out.

Whenever we are angry and don't express it appropriately, the anger comes back to hurt us. It's sort of like the kickback that happens when a shotgun is fired. Have you ever seen that? When a large gun goes off, it shoots the ammunition forward, but the gun also recoils backward from the force of the blast. If a gun isn't positioned correctly, it can do great damage—not only forward, but backward. When you don't know how to express anger appropriately, you shoot other people, but then anger's kickback wounds you as well.

Think about it: how might your anger have hurt people—or yourself?

» Perhaps you have fractured family relationships because of your anger.

» You may have lost an important business deal.

» Perhaps you've actually physically hurt another person. Or your anger caused someone else to blow up and he came after you. You got a bloody nose. Or maybe you talked your way out of it, but your kids saw it all happen, and the fear of the moment impacted them greatly.

» Maybe you struggle to maintain dating relationships because your anger flares up whenever you go over a relational speed bump.

» Some of you are having physical complications in your body because of the imploding stress caused by anger—headaches, hypertension, gluttony, irritable bowel syndrome.

» You might claim a personal relationship with Jesus, but friends and family are turned off to Jesus because of your anger. Your spiritual testimony falls on deaf ears because you can't control the rage you feel.

These are examples of emotional and relational consequences. I didn't even mention the stuff around your house that gets kicked, thrown, or broken.

So what do you do if you're stuck in anger? This is not who you want to be. You want to be a person who follows Christ wholeheartedly and lives the abundant life He promised. Your anger is keeping you from that. It's sidetracked you on your spiritual journey and derailed you from the life you know is best.

So how can you rise above anger? How can you have a fresh start today?

The Anger, the Rage, the Pain

Ungodly expressions of anger—and the results—affect everybody. It doesn't matter if you're young or old, male or female. Recently a woman told me, "I don't think this applies to me. Anger seems to be more of a guy thing." While she said this, her boyfriend was in the background, shaking his head and mouthing, "*Don't believe her.*"

The truth is that far too many interactions between people—friendships, business dealings, family relationships—are sources of pain, confusion, and even outright danger. Anger can take many forms. A huge problem is when anger results in a pattern of mistreatment, and climates of destruction are allowed to fester. This falls into the "abuse" category, and it must be stopped.

Ungodly anger may exhibit itself in a variety of ways, including:

» **physically**, where you inflict actual bodily pain or injury on another person;

» **verbally**, involving insults, cruel sarcasm, or put-downs that go far beyond good-natured joking;

» **psychologically**, where you intimidate others, or play mind games, or issue impossible expectations, or give ill-defined or constantly changing goals; it may involve social isolation, forced financial dependence, threats of bodily harm to others or yourself, or acts that elicit fear, such as destroying property or hurting pets;

» **sexually**, involving indecent exposure or coerced sexual acts; and

» **spiritually**—although we don't hear about this as much, it still happens. This is when spiritual authority is misused or biblical truths are twisted to justify hurt; it can come from a pastor, a church leader, a professor, a church member, a denomination—even from a certain neighborhood, town, or region in the country.

I want to show you two Bible verses that help shed God's light on anger, and what you can do about it if you suspect it's an issue in your life. You don't have to be stuck in this area. In response to anger, you can actually choose peace instead of pain—we'll talk about that in depth a little later on in this chapter. But first, let's go to God's Word. Ephesians 4:26–27 says, "Be angry but do not sin; do not let the sun go down on your anger, and give no opportunity to the devil" (RSV). The apostle Paul wasn't writing new wisdom here to the church of Ephesus. He was actually quoting from the Old Testament—Psalm 4:4—"Be angry, but sin not" (RSV).

Look at the first two words of both verses. Say them with me: *Be angry*. Does that surprise you? You have God's permission to be angry! Anger is okay. It's one of the many normal human emotions given to us from God. If you never got angry, you'd have no passion, opinions, or convictions. If you can honestly say you never feel any anger, please do yourself a favor and check the obituary for your own name. You might be dead, and you don't know it.

How can anger be a good thing—a thing that's okay with God? The key is to read the remainder of those verses. Neither of them stops at "Be angry." Like so many great passages in the Bible, these verses both contain a big "but." In these two verses it says be angry—*but* don't sin. Be angry—*but* deal with the anger before it turns ugly. Be angry—*but* don't allow your anger to open the door for the devil to walk through and use your anger to do his work.

The key is that godly anger always requires a godly response! I can think of at least two ways this is revealed in practical life:

Righteous Indignation

With this type of anger, I don't want to hurt someone; I want to help someone. For instance, when I hear about orphans in Haiti not having enough food to eat, that makes me angry. I feel a sense of injustice, and that anger fuels me to take action; I want to do something about it. That anger is godly, and it's okay to have it.

Jesus exhibited this type of anger in Matthew 21:12–14 when He threw the money changers out of the temple. These people were stealing from others, taking advantage of the poor, and desecrating the house of God. Christ felt righteously indignant because none of these hawkers had any concern or respect for God.

Response to Good but Frustrated Desires

If I long for something that's good and true and right, and my desires are not met, then I feel blocked, thwarted, let down, or frustrated. Anger is a normal emotional response (we might also feel grief), and it's not wrong—as long as our expression of it is godly.

Jesus showed this type of anger in Matthew 12:34 when He called the Pharisees a "brood of vipers." Jesus had just healed several people, but the Pharisees were overly concerned about keeping rules. We don't know the exact motivation for Jesus' strong words here, but from other places in Scripture, we know that He wanted all men to come to repentance (1 Tim. 2:4). Jesus wanted something for these Pharisees that was good and true and right, but instead they demonstrated what was sinful. That made Him angry. The so-called rulers of the law had no compassion for those who were suffering and in need of help. They were more interested in tying Jesus' hands with a strict set of impossible rules to follow. Christ was appalled at the fact that their hearts had become so hard. And His frustration with them was clear: "How will you escape being condemned to hell?" (Matt. 23:33).

These are, again, examples of godly responses to anger. But what if your responses are not so godly? You're stuck in a cycle of shamefully displayed anger. How do you get a fresh start? If you've been reading closely, you know that God has the power to change us—but our part in the process is also important. We have to *cooperate* with Him. So how do we do that? Ask yourself, when a stressful situation comes my way, how can I stand strong and hold out for truth while avoiding revenge and retaliation?

Choose Pain . . . or Choose Peace

There are two ways we can respond the next time we're angry: with pain or with peace. Anger always requires a response, and our choices lead either to more hurt or to godly reactions. On one hand, we can make a God-honoring response. On the other, we can respond in a way where the enemy wins. Let's take a look at both of these responses, beginning with the harmful one.

Response 1: Choosing Pain

The situation typically starts with some sort of irritation. The irritation produces feelings of anger. We let the anger simmer, or boil over and erupt, and we desire revenge. Sometimes we take this revenge; other times we just cultivate the feeling within ourselves. Usually, the feelings of revenge lead to hate at some level. Hate always leads to pain.

Over time, anger festers and becomes toxic in our souls. I don't want to spend much time on this response, mostly because we know it all too well. Besides, there's a better response than becoming a pawn in the devil's plans.

Response 2: Choosing Peace

Based on biblical wisdom and best practices, choosing peace is the correct way to respond to anger. When something irritating happens:

Don't deny it. Make a conscious decision to call an irritation what it is. Something's wrong. It's okay to say that. We've already seen in the

Ephesians passage that if you're authentically angry, you're just being a human being, and you can be thankful that your heart is still pumping. Anger itself is neutral—neither good nor evil. So we don't need to deny anger when it arrives.

I spoke with a guy this week who told me that he never allows his children to get angry because he was taught that anger is always bad. That's sad. Anger is a natural emotion. It's fine for all people—including kids—to express anger. It's how we choose to express it that can become harmful. Please don't live in denial. People sometimes want to spiritualize away anger. This is also a form of denial. It's when you say things like, "Oh, I don't get angry anymore. I'm a *Christian*." Look, I work with Christians every day. They get angry, believe me. People are people.

Delay your anger. When you first sense an irritation, acknowledging it is the first step. Saying something as simple as "Something's wrong here" is a very healthy action. Another healthy action that goes right along with that is *delaying* your anger. Put it on hold. That gives you the opportunity to say to yourself, "I could be wrong here, so let me think this through." This simple action requires a depth of maturity. This is where you need to slow the situation down to assess what's truly going on.

I read this week that some men like to delay their anger by getting in their car and driving. (That's nice. There's nothing more reassuring than an angry man behind the wheel. No wonder we have so much road rage these days.) The same research indicated that women, when angry, prefer to withdraw and eat. Now, that's more logical. And since I'm a man in touch with my feminine mystique, I do both. I drive to food. Taco Bell is just far enough away that I can cool down. And, if I'm really mad, you should see how fast they get me the chalupa. Whatever your positive delaying tactic is, do it—as long as it doesn't lead to rage (or gluttony). A better practice is to go for a walk. Or go to a room where you can be alone and think things out. Give yourself a time-out.

Here's how I've learned to delay my anger—with the conscious choice to be patient. Proverbs 16:32 says, "Patience is better than strength.

Controlling your temper is better than capturing a city" (NCV). I simply say to myself, "I could be wrong." That's it. Doing this very thing is proven to calm people down. "I could be wrong here. Maybe there's another side to this story. I could be wrong. I don't think I am. But I could be . . . "

Some of you haven't said these words for a long, long time. Let's try it, all together. (Are you still in that coffee shop or bookstore?) Just say this phrase out loud: "*I could be wrong.*" Some of you did not look happy when you said it. And of course this will not help you if you just holler it in a really ticked-off voice: "I COULD BE WRONG!" So, try it again. Only this time, smile and say it pleasantly: "I could be wrong." Don't you feel better now? No? Well, maybe this idea won't work for you . . . I *could* be wrong.

This sounds so easy, but taking the time to practice saying this small phrase throughout the week will help you. Get it into your system. Then, when anger appears, and the thermostat is moving up, don't deny it . . . just delay it. Change environments if necessary, but then force yourself to say, "I could be wrong."

Define it—then deliver it to God. Here's where the gold is! This is where the big learning happens for most of us. Do whatever you can to catch this one. Actually, it involves two actions, but they fit so closely together that I want to link them here as one.

Anger is actually a secondary emotion. Usually, before anger, you feel some sort of hurt. It may be frustration, disappointment, annoyance, betrayal, loneliness, or fear, but whichever, *something* has hurt your psyche. After that, the secondary emotion kicks in quickly—that's usually anger.

If you're going to respond to irritation in a God-honoring way, you need to step back and see what's underneath the anger. Kind of like pulling back the covers on a lumpy bed to see what's hiding underneath. If you don't, you're simply dealing with the surface reaction and not the root cause. So step back, and then ask yourself this simple question: "*Why am I really angry?*"

Most people never ask this question, and they immediately react to whatever has triggered their anger. The result is a life that is both superficial and damaging. I want to encourage you to reflect before you respond. If you miss this vital step, you tend to live in denial, or discount your anger, or blame other people, or fall into the trap of being the victim. You never dig up the real reason for your anger, and the real reason for your anger is where God wants to meet you.

Having God meet you in your emotion means simply having a conversation with Him about what's going on in your life. Talk to God about your hurt, your fear, your frustration, or whatever your underlying emotion is. It's as simple as saying something like, "God, this happened"—and tell Him about the event—"and now I'm so angry because it made me feel . . ." Then name your emotion. Were you afraid? Frustrated? Hurt? Tell Him all about it. And finally, ask Him for help. You need a connection with Him now more than ever.

Dietrich Bonhoeffer, a German pastor and author, wrote, "He who is alone with his sin is utterly alone."[1] But with God, you don't have to be alone. You just have to be honest.

Let's try this. I'll give you a couple of scenarios of anger, and you try to figure out the primary emotion underneath the anger. Okay? Then we'll look at some ways you could deliver this emotion to God.

Example #1: Let's say you're a single female dating someone. This afternoon the guy breaks up with you. He gives you that lame line, "I love you a lot . . . but as a friend, and I don't want our relationship to ruin our friendship. It's not you . . . it's *me.*"

Suddenly, you're very angry. You lash out at the now ex-boyfriend. You call him stupid and ugly (because you're not thinking logically) and say that you never want to see him again. Then you storm off, crying.

What might be going on underneath this outburst? What will happen if you ask this simple question: "Why am I really angry?"

Perhaps you're angry because you feel deeply hurt, rejected, discarded. And you wanted so badly for this relationship to work. Perhaps you feel embarrassed—you gave away too much of your heart. Perhaps you feel annoyed—this guy took a lot of time, energy, and effort. Maybe you feel disheartened—what you really want is to get married, but now you have to go back to square one and start again.

How might you deliver this to God?

Of course you pray, but you also may want to go to God's Word.

A verse like Philippians 4:19 fits well at this time: "My God shall supply all your need according to His riches in glory by Christ Jesus" (NKJV). In other words—God knows you're longing for a spouse, and He will meet your need in His time and His way. Just stay close to Him through the Word and prayer. He will bring it to pass.

Psalm 46:1–2 also comes to mind: "God is our refuge and strength, an ever-present help in trouble. Therefore we will not fear, though the earth give way." In other words, God is in control. We have nothing to fear. Not even rejection.

Example #2: You're going over to a friend's house for dinner, and your wife is running late. You were ready on time, but she's taking fifteen hours to put on her eyeliner. By the time she gets to the car, you've already missed the first three courses, and you're visibly angry.

What's underneath it? Ask yourself that question: "Why am I really angry?"

Chances are it's frustration. You're frustrated because of pace-of-life issues. You're a busy guy, and you can't understand how anyone around you can have a different set of priorities and timetable.

How might God meet you in your frustration? How might you deliver this to God?

Again, go to God's Word in prayer. You may be legitimately frustrated by your wife's time-consuming eyeliner habit. Still, Scripture says, "Husbands, love your wives" (Eph. 5:25). Start there. In this situation, ask the Lord what would be the most *loving* thing you can do for your wife. It may be gentle confrontation. Perhaps she has a problem with time management, so your goal is to build her up in this area, not tear her down. Perhaps you simply need to be patient with your spouse. Maybe the most loving thing you can do for your wife is to swallow your sarcasm, smile when she gets in the car, and compliment her on how she looks. She's obviously spent a lot of time getting ready for this occasion.

Example #3: One directly from the Fields family (oh yeah, like the last one wasn't!): It's the middle of the night, and my wife wakes me up because she hears something downstairs. She says, "Doug, I heard something! Go downstairs and check it out!"

I'm barely awake at that point, and I'm thinking that my sweet wife probably fell asleep watching the news about some homicidal maniac who escaped from a maximum-security penitentiary for the criminally insane, and she thinks he's found our house. Besides, even if it is Hannibal Lecter rummaging around in our refrigerator, what good will I do anyway going down there in my BVDs, armed with a plunger and a clock radio?

So I roll over and say to Cathy, "I don't hear anything! Why don't you go down there?"

"Be the man!" my wife hisses at me.

Now we're both wide awake and staring at each other angrily in the dark.

A minute later we realize that the dog (who is a sleepwalker) accidentally bumped the remote, and he's now watching Animal Planet. But we're both still ticked at each other. We're angry. What was the issue?

We each need to ask ourselves, "Why am I angry?" and then deliver what we're feeling to the Lord. He will meet us where we are.

You can do the surmising here. I'll spare you all the details of our married life, but let's just conclude with this: if we never ask, "Why am I *really* angry?" we'll just be dealing with the surface issue, not the root issue.

Once the reason for being angry is defined and given over to the Lord, it can be properly dealt with, which brings us to the final action.

Defuse the situation—and diffuse your anger. This is when you actually respond in a way that honors God. You're not giving the devil an opportunity to use you to do his work. (Remember, anger always requires a response, and my choice is either pain or peace.) You're *defusing* the situation.

How do you defuse anger? Usually once you uncover the primary emotion, and the Lord meets you there with Scripture, the anger is defused naturally as God speaks into your life. But sometimes the anger still remains. You've uncovered the real problem, but the irritation still exists. What do you do then?

To defuse means you "remove the fuse from."[2] In other words, you make the situation less harmful, potent, or intense, just as you would by physically removing the fuse from a bomb. To put it another way, let's take a look at the homonym *diffuse*. If you *diffuse* your anger, you pour it out like a liquid. Light can be diffused to create a softer effect in a room. And your anger can be diffused by mixing it with actions that will produce peace.

Whenever you choose to defuse (and diffuse) anger, you are choosing to seek relational peace. You're taking to heart the words of verses such as Romans 12:18: "If possible, so far as it depends on you, be at peace with all men," (NASB) or Proverbs 15:1, "A gentle answer turns away wrath."

What are some practical ways of defusing the situation?

>> Ignore a negative comment. Just walk away. This instantly makes the situation less harmful. You're not there!

>> Don't reply to a person's irritating e-mail. All the words you probably think of are along the lines of *jerk, burn in hell, idiot, stupid, fool, nutball,* and *toilet plunger.* Choose, instead, godly silence—and hit Delete.

>> Back away, and don't pursue a fight, even though you know you're right.

» Let that psycho driver go on down the freeway after he just cut you off. Face it: there will always be nutty drivers in the world. You don't need to teach every one a lesson.

» Take a deep breath and then say nothing when a harsh reaction begs to spill from your lips.

» Go to the gym and work out your anger on the treadmill— even though you're angry as a hornet and would rather sting!

» Make a joke of things. Someone said something wrong, but laugh it off instead of blowing up. There will always be idiots in the world. You can stay cool when you make a joke of things.

» Stand your ground briefly, then walk away. Even though someone said the world's most hurtful thing to you, respond with a flat, "That's the most absurd thing I've ever heard." Or simply say to yourself, "I don't own that." Then walk away, exposing the other person's sin for what it is.

After you've *defused* the situation, one of the best ways of *diffusing* anger is to let some time go by. Then, once you're confident that your anger has scattered safely away, communicate clearly what caused you to be angry to the person who made you angry. But remember, it's important to let some time pass so you go through the steps of defining your anger. Then you can calmly express it in terms of hurt, fear, frustration, or whatever the emotion is.

When you do go to talk with the person who angered you, start your sentence with the word *I*. And I'm not talking about "I am so ticked off" either, but rather, "I *felt* . . . " and then tell the person what your true emotion was. This can be a calm conversation, where you own your hurt, fear, or frustration. For example, you can say, "I felt scared in that situation. My fear triggered anger, and I want to get to the bottom of this with you." Deal with it, and if fresh anger arises, defuse it quickly, so it doesn't reignite.

A Fresh View

Anger is a part of life, and it requires a response. But whenever we feel angry, we have a choice. We can take either the route that leads to pain, or the one that leads to peace. With God's help, we can choose peace and be on the way to a fresh start.

Can you imagine how different your life might be if your response to anger was to delight God? Can you see how your business relationships would be different? How your friendships might be stronger? If you're dating someone, how your conflicts might be less intense? If you're married, how your connection with your spouse would be more intimate, and your bond with your children deeper and more fulfilling? It would be so different with everybody in your life!

God can help you move from being stuck in anger to a fresh start today with everyone who knows you. Go to Him in prayer. Ask for His help in transforming you in this area. He will change your life when you yield it to Him.

Months from now, I can imagine people in your life who want to know why you're living and acting so differently. I can see people looking at your life and saying things like, "There's so much peace in you these days—what happened? You used to fly off the handle. You were the temper-tantrum queen. What's the source of that peace? Where does it come from? Please tell me how I can have it too!" I can see that! I can see that for you. I can see that for me. I can see that for your friends. People need the hope and help of God in their lives, because it changes them, right before the very eyes of those who knew them before.

Want to overcome your anger? Start today. In fact, if you do, I guarantee that soon enough you will have opportunities to put God's Word into action. Anticipate that over the next few days. When you feel anger coming on within you . . . don't do what you used to do that doesn't work. Respond in a way that leads to freedom and peace. You can do it. God wants to help.

Will you pray this prayer with me?

Dear God, I know there is so much pain in people's lives. But meanwhile, I've marked my life with anger that has wounded the people in my life even more, and the kickback is killing me. And God, I don't want to continue in the same angry direction. I need Your Word to come alive in me and help me to not sin in my anger. I don't want to give the devil any opportunity to use my actions for his glory. But in my own strength, I know I'll fail. God, I beg for Your strength! Give me the wisdom and the power to choose a response that leads to peace. May I find victory in my anger. I want to be changed by Your love. Thank You for loving me today . . . regardless. Amen.

CHAPTER 11

SHARING YOUR FRESH-START STORY

We've looked at a lot of personal issues in this book so far that can keep us from living God's best: hurt, anger, rejection, and so on. There's one more area I'd like to touch on that is different from these. Unlike hurt or anger, this additional area of our lives is not necessarily a struggle (although it might be considered a fear), yet it significantly affects those types of issues. It's how we care for others. If we really want to live life differently, to accelerate spiritual growth, and to get a fresh start on our spiritual journeys, we must learn to care for other people's spiritual condition.

When I use the word *care*, I'm referring to something deeper than simply being nice to people. Don't get me wrong—I'm supportive of nice. Nice is nice. I appreciate it when someone opens the door for me or pulls out my chair. Hey, if you're not a nice person . . . the DMV is always hiring.

But caring for others involves something much more than being nice. In this chapter I want to challenge you to learn to really care for someone's spiritual condition, to care about his connection with God, to care enough to make sure she knows about the good news of forgiveness and eternal life.

You might be thinking, *Wait, but I hang around a lot of people who aren't Christians.* Well, that's perfect! That's who I'm inviting you to care for—people who don't yet experience all that life has to offer through Jesus Christ.

I know that whenever I raise this subject, people instantly throw a lot of blockers in the way. It's not popular these days to talk about evangelism. Many Christians don't even like that word anymore. We're all just supposed to live and let live and allow everyone to find his or her own belief system. Or maybe you've been burned by folks who were obnoxious with their beliefs. Someone goofy has knocked on your door and wanted to sell you some kind of religion—and you don't want to be anything like that person. Or you've seen some crazy dude on TV with huge, poofy hair, sweating and gyrating all over the stage as he screams about the "love of Jesus." And that's just not you; thankfully, it's not me either.

Let me just say that I'm not going to ask you in this chapter to do anything fanatical. In fact, if it's easier for you, I want you to put aside the word *evangelism* if there's too much negative baggage connected to it.

Instead, I'm inviting you to fall increasingly in love with God. That's the plan. Fall in love with all His majesty and glory and goodness. Get to know the Savior as never before. When that happens, Scripture says that the love of Christ will compel you (2 Cor. 5:14). When we know God intimately, this gives us a new power to care for the spiritual condition of others. God has given us a fresh start. Now, part of the depth connected to a fresh start is allowing others to hear about or see the Power behind the fresh start. That's where our spiritual stories come into play.

When you share your transformational story, others can be exposed to an option that can move them from stuck to starting anew . . . with a Power that is greater than their own. Let's talk more about what that looks like in real life.

Conversations about God

What I'm about to say may surprise you—it surprises a lot of Christians. Here we go: Non-Christians are *not* afraid to have conversations about God. They're seldom afraid of Jesus either. Usually, they're just afraid of Christians. And that's the problem we all encounter. They're worried we might lay hands on them and attempt an exorcism. They're afraid of weird Christians who are pushy, preachy, and phony. And that's not what I'm asking you to be.

Let's look at this more in depth. According to a recent Gallup poll, just under 80 percent of Americans believe in God.[1] And 82 percent of those people call themselves Christians.[2]

But it's my experience that a high percentage of people who call themselves Christians don't use a Bible-based definition. When you drill down to their definition, you find that they call themselves Christian because they either (1) were born in the United States, (2) went to church as a child and sang "This Little Light of Mine," (3) were born into a Christian family, or (4) have the last name *Christian*.

Frankly, those actions don't make someone a Christian any more than being born in a Taco Bell makes someone a chalupa. So what is a Christian, really?

According to Acts 11:26, Antioch was the first place where people began to be called "Christians." So who were these folks, and what made them "Christian"? Simply, they were believers in Christ (hence, the *Christ-* in *Christians*). That is, they *believed* beyond a shadow of a doubt that Jesus was who He said He was—the Son of God who came to earth to die for their sins.

Today, as then, belief in Jesus Christ and in the work He did for us on the cross is the point on which true Christianity hinges. It's John 3:16 in a nutshell.

Here's some encouraging news: if almost 80 percent of Americans believe in God, most of the work in sharing your story is already done. What remains is helping people move from a casual, distant belief in an impersonal God to an up-close, personal, and passionate relationship with a living Savior, His Son. Whenever you help people move forward spiritually, your own life takes on a new meaning and purpose. The old things that drag you down just don't receive as much focus. Your spiritual growth doesn't stagnate anymore. You have a fresh perspective as to where you're headed and what's really important.

Now, I know that some of you are having thoughts like these:

>> *I'm just going to skip this chapter, Doug. Thanks. That stuff about managing anger was fine, but I don't think this applies to me.*

>> *I'm not good at telling others about Jesus. I don't think it's my spiritual gift.*

>> *How could I possibly help others spiritually? The fish just fell off my car bumper.*

Let me begin with a confession: I also have apprehensions about talking to people about Jesus. I know you might find that hard to believe since my job involves getting up on stage and talking about Christ, but, strangely enough, I find that much easier than speaking to someone one-on-one. If people reject me on stage, I just look around the room at someone else. Crowds can be comfortable that way. But one-on-one . . . that's not as comfortable for me. My natural reaction is to clam up and keep things to myself.

I know some Christians who are regularly leading strangers to Jesus. When they tell me their stories, I always feel so guilty in comparison. I feel like a spiritual reject. I begin to think that even cults wouldn't want me. I may not even be good enough for Amway.

For instance, I have a friend who makes it his goal to get into a spiritual conversation every time he gets on an airplane. He's amazing. But whenever I get on an airplane, I just want to sleep. When I sit next to people and they ask me what I do for a living, I say, "I'm a pastor." Guess what? As soon as they hear that, they usually want to sleep too, or they claim they got on the wrong plane, or they ask the flight attendant to seat them next to an atheist.

Don't get me wrong. I'm not embarrassed about my relationship with God or ashamed of the message of the good news. I just feel more comfortable with a different delivery system. What about you? If this was a book where I said that in order to embrace your own fresh start you need to learn obscure Bible verses, dress in military garb, memorize canned responses to questions, then race out to the nearest Wal-Mart parking lot and tell strangers they're going to hell . . . would you still be reading?

Let's put this into perspective: Instead of strangers, you have people in your life you are already close to, have relationships with, and care about. You want them to know and experience God's unconditional love for them—but it's just plain scary to talk to them about Jesus. Those are the people I'm inviting you to focus on most.

What do you do? Having spiritual conversations freaks you out. But you know that people have a deep need for what Jesus can bring. So how can you move from feeling stuck in fear to a fresh start in this area of your life?

Like the Woman at the Well

Some of the last words Jesus spoke contain a challenge to care about others' eternity. In Matthew 28:19, Jesus said, "Go and make disciples of all the nations" (NLT). So how do you do that without being pushy, preachy, or phony? If there was a way to have a spiritual conversation with someone you know and care about that was nonthreatening, natural, and focused on love rather than an agenda to convert, would you be interested?

A great example of a natural conversation is one that took place between Jesus and a Samaritan woman. It's found in John 4:1–42. Jesus left Judea to return to Galilee. The Bible says, "He had to go through Samaria on the way" (v. 4 NLT). If you read that line too fast, you'll miss the humor in it. No Jewish person *had* to go through Samaria. Staunch, law-abiding Jews did everything they could to avoid any contact with these people whom they referred to as "Samaritan dogs." There was huge racial tension between the Jews and Samaritans—they hated each other. But Jesus "had" to go there! What does that say about Jesus?

About noon, Jesus sat down at a well in Samaria. He was tired from His long walk. Jesus was alone at the time, because His disciples had gone into the village to buy food. Along came a Samaritan woman to draw water. Jesus asked her for a drink.

Now, in that desert culture, women would typically draw water in the morning because it was cooler. Women weren't usually alone at this place either. Drawing water was a social event for all the women of the community. A trip to the well meant a chance to chat, swap stories, and catch up on the latest news of the town. But this woman was alone at noontime—the hottest part of the day. None of the other women would be there. Why? The woman didn't fit. She wore the scarlet letter.

The woman was surprised when Jesus talked to her, noting that Jews don't usually have anything to do with Samaritans. She asked Him why He wanted a drink. She was surprised because Jesus broke just about every barrier to engage her. He broke the racial barrier (Jew/Samaritan). He broke the gender barrier (in that culture, men didn't casually talk with women). He also broke a social barrier (she was immoral and shunned). I like to imagine the scene this way: Jesus probably had strong Jewish features, not like today's Hollywood portrayal of Him, with blue eyes or light brown hair. If Jesus looked like He does in our movies, the woman might have said, "I am a Samaritan and you're a Swede—*yahoody.*"

Here's where Jesus went to work. He said, "People soon become thirsty again after drinking this water. But the water I give them takes away thirst altogether. It becomes a perpetual spring within them, giving them eternal life."

Jesus took something that was common to the woman (her thirst) and started a spiritual conversation about it. Everyone is thirsty for something. Thirsty for a relationship. Thirsty for power. Thirsty for respect or value or fame or money. You name it, but everyone is thirsty for something. We will keep drinking different solutions, attempting to quench our thirsts. But Jesus said, "I've got what will make you never feel thirsty again."

Then Jesus went deeper. He asked the woman to go and get her husband. Uh-oh, only one problem. "I don't have a husband," the woman replied.

"That's right," Jesus said. "You don't have a husband—you've had five husbands, and you aren't even married to the man you're living with now."

Hello! Can you imagine the spiritual whiplash from that little insight? If she had been taking a drink right then, she probably would've sprayed water all over Jesus. That feeling of being caught in a lie is so uncomfortable. There's no getting out of it. Your mind is working fast trying to buy some time, desperately hoping you can come up with a good cover story.

So she tried a different tack. She changed the subject and asked a question about where Jews worship. This is a classic redirect. "Hey Jesus, look over there! Is that a chicken? Let's not focus on my sexual history . . . let's talk about something that's really been bugging me . . . where our ancestors worshipped . . . that has always troubled me . . . yeah, that's right . . . ancestral worship."

Do we ever do that? Conversations get a little too close to truth, sensitive spots are revealed, sin is exposed, and we redirect the conversation. It's much easier to see faults in others rather than in ourselves.

The conversation at the well ended with Jesus showing the woman that He was indeed the Messiah she had been longing for. He quenched the thirst she had continually experienced. The woman evidently received the truth—or was close to it—because she went back into the village and invited everyone: "Come and meet a man who told me everything I ever did!"

Here's where the teaching about caring for others really kicks in for us. After the woman left, the disciples came back from buying food and urged Jesus to eat, but He refused. Why? Because He wanted to use the moment to speak into the disciples' lives. He wanted to speak to them about higher things—heavenly things. The disciples undoubtedly couldn't understand why Jesus didn't want to eat. They were famished, and He had been on the same journey as they had.

Instead, Jesus said to His disciples: "My nourishment comes from doing the will of God. . . . Look around you! Vast fields are ripening all around us and are ready now for the harvest. . . . The fruit [we can] harvest is people brought to eternal life. What joy awaits both the planter and the harvester alike!" (vv. 34–36 NLT).

In essence, Jesus was saying, "I just got nourished. I just did what I came to do, and it's so fulfilling. Forget about the falafel. Did you just see that woman I was talking to? Did you see the look in her eyes? Did you catch the emptiness of her soul? Couldn't you see the potential in her life? Can you see how her painful decisions don't have to define her anymore? Her life is going to be different. She's got a fresh start! That's the nourishment I'm talking about."

This is the same message Christ has for us today. There are a lot of people just like the woman at the well who need an encounter with Jesus. They don't need religion and rules; they need Jesus. The time is ripe—they're everywhere. And great joy awaits you if you care about their spiritual condition.

A Way to Care

Let's make this personal. How do we actually go about the business of spiritually caring for people? We could all point to people in our lives who need Jesus. So now what? How do we begin to care for them and engage them in spiritual conversations?

Remember that God always does the ultimate work in changing anyone's life—including ours. We yield ourselves to Him through the Word and by prayer, and then He gets us unstuck. He provides the POWER; we provide the cooperation. But there are several things we can do that are part of cooperating with God so that we can engage *with* Him in His plan.

Following are some specific actions we can take to cooperate with God in this area. I've built them around something I knew I could remember—the acronym CARE. That's what Jesus did. He *cared*. Let's look at each of these actions:

Capitalize on Common Ground

What was a common starting place for a spiritual conversation between Jesus and the woman at the well? Water! Jesus took advantage of what they were both there for. The conversation started at the well, then moved from water and thirst to spiritual truth.

Your common ground is wherever you're regularly with people. For you, it could be your workplace, a sporting event, the school your kids attend, a restaurant you frequent, or the flat-screen section at Wal-Mart.

I have a friend who has been a coach for thirty years and a follower of Jesus for even longer, and he meets other coaches at a local watering hole twice a month. That's his common ground. His conversation there doesn't need to be limited to "tastes great" and "less filling" or offense/defense. He can begin *spiritual* conversations where he meets people on common ground.

When you know you have things in common, it's a lot easier for conversation to happen. The common ground brings you together. Take advantage of that. This action is a simple one. Start with where you feel most comfortable.

Accept People Where They Are

Personally, I find this one of the biggest hurdles in having spiritual conversations. It's so easy for me to throw up a wall of judgment because of someone's lifestyle or choices. I confess I do this whenever I see middle-aged Orange County men who have toupees and drive sports cars and wear gold chains and open their shirts to show their chest hair. I'm like, "Who are you trying to kid, bud?!"

But that's a man who needs Christ in his life. As soon as I judge him, I create a me-versus-you mentality. Instead of having a free-flowing conversation with someone, I'm thinking about the obvious midlife crisis he's having, the pungent aftershave smell on his lapels, and the "I shop at the Gap" tattoo on his arm. A wall goes up, and conversation goes down. Whenever I don't accept people, I won't care for them. And that's a problem.

This is very real—and I'm not the only one who fights it. Most non-Christians I've talked to have told me that when they talk to Christians, they sense an "I'm-okay-you're-not-okay" attitude. That grieves me. If you're not a Christian and you have experienced that from another Christian, I am so sorry.

Accepting someone as he is doesn't mean you have to agree with his lifestyle or approve of his choices. You just accept him as a person—God's creation. When Jesus interacted with the woman at the well, He didn't say, "Hi, I'm Jesus the Messiah. I already know who you are—you're the town tramp. I'm disgusted by your blatant disregard for the laws of marriage, and if you weren't so sleazy, I'd tell you about a kind of water that would quench your thirst. But I can't do that. You're too messed up. Have a good day, now. Hey, disciples—where's My lunch!?"

It's quite the challenge to learn to see other people through Christ's eyes. But it's the secret to acceptance.

Risk Sharing Your Spiritual Story

When I was a new Christian, I was taught to share the entire message of the Bible in thirty seconds in case I ever had someone trapped in the elevator. The agenda was convert, convert, convert. Success was "closing the deal." It never worked—not that I knew of, anyway. I'd still be on Genesis chapter 2 by the time the elevator got going again.

Instead of making conversion your goal, make the goal a spiritual conversation where you simply care enough to ask questions and engage in dialogue with someone. If that feels too tough, start with a single spiritual statement or a question or two, and see what happens from there.

That's kind of what Jesus did. He made a spiritual statement to the woman. It was an awesome one: *I am the Messiah.* Your statement should be a little different, but even a small spiritual statement requires courage and vulnerability. Depending on the context of your common ground, the statements could sound like one of these:

» "A group of friends and I are studying the Bible, and we're learning about Jesus' life. It's really interesting."
» "At the church I go to, we're trying to figure out what on earth we're here for. I know life is short. I don't want to waste mine."
» "No, I'm not dating anyone right now. I'm waiting for God's timing and for the right person for my life. I trust that God will provide."
» "I used to have a problem with drugs or alcohol [or a bad marriage or anger or any of a million other human struggles], but aligning my life with Jesus has given me a brand-new life."

Put things into your own words, obviously. It doesn't have to be much. You don't have to have it all together to have a spiritual conversation. Just ask questions, or tell your story, or bits of your story, and point the conversation to Jesus. That kind of honesty and transparency, spoken one-on-one with another person on common ground, can be very powerful.

You may not realize the power of your story or the influence you can have with it, but you have a story to share, and there is no one who can tell it better than you! Chances are, you are a lot more inspiring than you give yourself credit for. There are people out there who need to hear your story for hope, healing, encouragement, and direction to God.

Jesus knew the concept of story. He understood that God has ordered the universe as one big narrative. It has a beginning, middle, and end. And our very own lives are individual storylines within God's bigger narrative. That means your story has a place in God's story. You *are* in a story. A great story—you just may not realize it. Humans are wired for stories. We respond best to tales that include forgiveness, redemption, resurrection, do-overs, new births, and fresh starts. It's like we all have six guitar strings running through our souls, and when they get plucked with these themes, they reverberate with God's truth and make the sounds of meaning come alive within us.

Have you ever thought about what your spiritual story is? Basically, it involves just two components:

» What was my life like before Jesus?
» What has it been like since Jesus?

Let me just address what some may be undoubtedly thinking—*My story is boring!* Sometimes when I hear other people's "radical" stories and I compare them to my vanilla, plain, young-child-becomes-a-Christian story, I think, *Wow . . . if only I had done drugs, been shot in a gang fight, or gotten a tattoo of a pit bull fighting Elvis on one side of my neck, then*

I'd really have a story. But I've learned that my life-change story doesn't need to be intense in order to have impact.

>> I didn't need a painful past to recognize that I was totally empty without Jesus.
>> I didn't need to murder someone to know what a heart of darkness felt like.
>> I didn't have to be an atheist to know what it's like to doubt.
>> I didn't have to be kidnapped to understand what loneliness and fear are like.
>> I didn't have to spend time in jail to know how it felt to be imprisoned by sin.
>> I didn't have to knock over a bicyclist to know what it is like to have an evil heart.

When I'm in conversation with someone on common ground, I'll often use my story to get into his story. I tell my story, then ask a simple question at the end. I usually say something like this:

> *I never intended to be a pastor. I wanted to be a professional athlete, but I wasn't good at anything. In high school a buddy invited me to church and told me there would be a comedian and a lot of cute girls. I was all over that. After the comedian finished, he said, "How many of you love to laugh?" I shot my hand straight up. He asked, "How many of you would like to experience laughter all the time." Once again, straight up. Then he taught me the difference between laughter and joy and how laughter dries up and joy doesn't. How joy comes from having a relationship with God. All I had ever heard about was religion. I was curious about a relationship with God . . . and that's when my journey of faith started.*
>
> *What about you? Have you ever had any interest in God?*

It's not preachy, pushy, or phony. It's just my story.

You have a story too. And the person you're talking with has a story. And God has a story of love and wants to connect His story with the person's story and begin writing a new story: *Before Jesus; after Jesus.*

Expect God to Do His Part

The goal in caring for others spiritually is to be faithful. Faithfulness is more important than results. God doesn't need you to get His results. He's always ultimately in control.

Often people say things like, "God really needs me to reach that person!" But the truth is that God doesn't actually need you—He doesn't *need* you for anything. God wasn't stumped when He created the universe, and He can certainly get along without your help now.

But He does invite you into His plans. He asks if you want to join Him in His work. That's the opportunity! When He uses you to be a link in the life of another person's spiritual eternity, you'll never be the same. Talk about a fresh start! The benefit is as much yours as it is the other person's.

There's great comfort in knowing that if someone doesn't respond to the love of God, the message of forgiveness, and the hope for eternity, it doesn't mean you're a failure. You're not a loser if he or she doesn't "convert." That's not your job. Your job is to be faithful to care. That's it. From then on, expect and depend on God to do His part.

When God is involved, incredible things happen. Look at what happened because of the woman at the well. After she told her fellow villagers all about Christ, they came out to see Him and begged Him to stay. Jesus stayed for two days, long enough for many of them to hear His message and believe. They didn't believe because of the woman. They believed because of Jesus.

We don't have to have all the answers. We just need to be faithful in caring for people and see what God does.

Unstuck in Your Story

One final point: Some of you are undoubtedly saying, "But what if I have a spiritual conversation with someone and he asks me something I don't know the answer to? What will I do then?"

If you're asked a difficult question about God, doctrine, theology, or whatever, it's perfectly okay to say, "I wish I knew the answer to that, but I don't." Maybe you'll help that person find the answer later. Maybe it's okay simply to let some things be.

The important thing to remember is that people are hurting and can benefit from hearing of your experiences with Jesus. People in pain need to hear that they're not alone and that someone else has made it out from underneath the pile. People who are lonely need to hear about how you've found community. People who live without a relationship with God need to hear that life is so much better when they discover it's not all about them—it's about God. People who are caught in a lifestyle of sin and darkness need to hear the story of someone who lived there and found the light.

Sharing personal stories about Jesus reveals the power of God. You don't have to be a perfect Christian or have everything together. God invites you to be in process—and perhaps, along the way, help someone else get a fresh start. When that happens, hold on . . . you're in for a spiritual growth ride of your life.

CHAPTER 12

WHAT YOU VALUE MOST

O n September 18, 2007, computer science professor Randy Pausch stepped in front of an audience of four hundred people at Carnegie Mellon University to deliver a lecture titled "Really Achieving Your Childhood Dreams." The talk was modeled after an ongoing series of lectures in which top academics are asked to ponder what matters most, and then give a hypothetical "final talk" (e.g., "What wisdom would you try to impart to the world if you knew it was your last chance?").

What was different about Pausch's last lecture was that the clock was truly ticking rapidly for him. With slides of his CT scans beaming out to the audience, Randy told his audience about the cancer that was devouring his pancreas and that would ultimately claim his life in a matter of months. On the stage that day, Randy appeared youthful, energetic, often cheerful, and darkly funny. An ironic image, perhaps, of someone who seemed so invincible but was so near the end of his time on earth.

Randy's speech became a phenomenon. The lecture was videotaped, posted on the Internet, and viewed more than a million times in the first month after its delivery. The simple message seemed to captivate the world. Randy appeared on *The Oprah Winfrey Show* and all the major news outlets. He went on to write a book called *The Last Lecture* based on the same principles of the speech. The book appeared at the top of the New York Times Best Seller List for many months.

Sadly, Randy lost his battle with pancreatic cancer on July 25, 2008. Yet his question about what matters most continues to inspire us, and prompts us to ask the same types of questions: If you knew the clock was ticking rapidly for you, what would become most important in your life? What would you value most? If you had one month to live, what would you do?

The question, what do you value most? is a particularly great one because it forces us to articulate our current values. It's the final thought I want to leave you with in this book. How do *you* answer the question, what do I value most? Truly, when we think a little deeper about it, we realize this isn't really a hypothetical question. The clock *is* ticking. Death is inevitable for all humanity. It's not a matter of *if* we die; it's a matter of *when*. So when we articulate our top values, we are able to see what we've come to hold as important. Some of our values may appear noble in this new light—we're glad we spend time working to uphold them. Other values may appear not so noble. We wonder how we could misplace effort and energy on something so unworthy.

The aim of this final chapter is to help you examine your values as they truly are. Then I'd like for you to ask yourself if you are stuck in the pursuit of some unimportant values. Are you truly valuing the things you need to be? Or are you floundering?

Keep reading. We'll ask—and answer—these questions together.

Who Wants to Think about Death?

I need to begin by admitting I'm kind of creeped out by thinking about death, in the sense that it's not too far away. I'm sure a little counseling would help me get to the bottom of why just thinking about death seems to freak me out.

It may go back to when I was a child and had several near-death experiences. I was so close to death once that I was actually offered last rites in the middle of a street after I fell off my bike. It wasn't an ordinary fall, mind you—it was a near-death fall. Do you remember Schwinn bicycles? When I was a kid, if you had one in my neighborhood, you were among the privileged, the rich, the spoiled. Most of the kids on my street owned Schwinns. At least it felt like they all did. All except me. I had a Huffy—Kmart's brand. You couldn't be cool with a Huffy, but that was my life—no expensive brands for me. My friends all had the Spalding indoor/outdoor leather basketballs, and I had one from the grocery store that looked like a volleyball painted brown. My buddies wore Levis; I wore Sears' brand—and huskies, at that. Huskies on a Huffy. Notice the repeated letter *h*? Must have been a code for *humiliation*. All I needed was a lop-eared dog named Happy to make me a total geek.

In order not to get beat up for my geekiness, I had to compensate. I became the block champion of riding wheelies. A wheelie is when you pull up the front tire and ride balanced on the back tire for as far as you can. No kid on a Schwinn could ride a wheelie farther than Mr. H. Huffy. Whenever I made my friends look bad, they would be poor losers and say, "That Huffy is made out of plastic and doesn't weigh as much as our bikes." I'd then jump on their Schwinns and prove them wrong. I was the Evel Knievel of the Huffy posse.

Well, one time I jumped on my friend's ten-speed Schwinn and forgot that ten-speeds had different braking systems than traditional Huffy Stingrays. I pulled up to do a wheelie and pulled up too far. I went to apply the foot brakes to balance out—but there were no foot brakes! The bike came over backward on top of me, and I slammed my head on the concrete. Luckily, my husky pants hit first and saved me from serious brain damage.

Let me go on record here and state that I grew up in the pre–bike helmet era. Mandatory bicycle helmets were introduced much later on, into what is now known as the "Era of Overprotective Everything." As a kid, I wouldn't be caught dead with a helmet (although I was almost caught dead without one). Mind you, if we had been forced to wear helmets back then, I am positive that I would not have had a cool one. I'd be the kid wearing a hard hat from the hardware store.

Anyway, with my friend's bike now on top of me, I lay on the street with blood gushing out the back of my head. I knew I was dying. Things began to go dark, and I had a vision of a weaker generation legislating bike helmets. Two strangers pulled over. One asked, "Are you okay?"

"Yeah," I said, "if losing five pints of blood a minute is normal. No, I'm not okay! I'm dying!"

The other guy said (seriously), "You don't want to die yet, because I bet you're still a virgin." (This reveals the value system of the male mind, by the way—you are not allowed to die if you've never had sex.) I was only ten years old—I had no idea if I was or wasn't a virgin. I thought a virgin was a state on the East Coast.

"I go to a Catholic school," the other guy said, "so I can administer last rites if you really think you're going to die."

"Yes, please," I said. I had no idea what those were, but I figured if God was somehow involved, I had better get them administered quickly. So the guy did. Then my dad came over, yanked me up by the belt, and told me to shake it off and get in the house. So, I guess I wasn't really dying.

That's all I remember about death as a kid. Now, as an adult, I'm not so much afraid of death. But I just don't like to think about it. I go to any extreme to avoid the conversation. For instance, when Cathy and I were first married, we'd be at the beach or somewhere, and out of the blue she'd ask something like, "If I died, would you get remarried?"

"What?" I'd say. "I don't even want to talk about it!"

Then, just to taunt me, she'd say, "Well, if you died, I'd get remarried right away. In fact, I'd look hot at your funeral."

I couldn't stand it. I'd jump up and go for a swim. I just couldn't talk about the subject of death.

Are you like me that way—you don't like to think about death? It's okay. Even though I don't like the subject much, death is a reality for all of us. It's headed our way. No matter how rich, powerful, or successful we are, mortality is the great equalizer. Warren Buffet, Bill Gates, Donald Trump . . . guess what? They're all on limited time, just like the rest of us. (Trump already looks like he gets his hair styled at a mortuary.)

When my dad died a while back, it rocked my world. I was stunned. Dads aren't supposed to die. Of course, it's not like I didn't see it coming. I did. He had Parkinson's disease, and I watched him deteriorate. But the finality of his death did something to me. It fast-forwarded my thinking to the deeper places about life, my purpose, my future, my legacy. It really hit me how temporary this life is. When I was under forty, I don't believe I ever thought about death until my dad was diagnosed. I figured that since I was such a fine physical specimen, I'd live to ninety, which seemed so far away. Today, at the strapping age of forty-six, my life is probably more than half over. I'm in my second half already, but in some ways I feel like I'm just getting started. It seems like only yesterday I was riding wheelies in my neighborhood.

Man, how time flies.

Thinking about Time

There's one fallacy about death that I'd like to dispel: it's the phrase I just wrote—that *time flies*. We hear that expression a lot; it's even become part of our default vernacular when we're busy, but really it's not true.

Time doesn't fly. Time is one of the few constants we can rely on. Inflation doesn't affect time. And recession doesn't affect it either. Five minutes today is the same as five minutes was twenty years ago, and it's the same as five minutes will be twenty years in the future. Time never flies. But it does tick away. And once it's gone, we'll never get it back.

There's a Bible verse that puts this in perspective for us. James 4:14 says, "How do you know what will happen tomorrow? For your life is like the morning fog—it's here a little while, then it's gone" (NLT). What's this verse saying? It's an encouragement for us to pay attention to how short life is. Instead of blaming time as though it has a will of its own, we need to take responsibility and be good stewards of the time God gives us.

To do this we need help. This is where a prayer like the one found in Psalm 90:12 comes into play: "Teach us to make the most of our time, so that we may grow in wisdom" (NLT).

That verse summarizes the theme of this book. We don't want to be people stuck in whatever is holding us back. We want to live each day with the newness and abundance of life that Christ offers us. My prayer for us all throughout this book has been: *God, help us identify the true values in life—what matters most—and then give us the power to spend our time on those values.*

Without living out that prayer, many of us will squander our lives pursuing the values of the world. We'll clutch and crawl after things that look good on the outside, but they'll only leave us hollow and empty within. We can't have it both ways. We either pursue God's values or the world's. That's why it's so important as we close this book to examine what we truly value. As with all other things, it is God who does the real work in aligning our priorities; He transforms us into who He wants us to be. But as I've said so often in this book, we are given responsibility in the process as well. We are responsible to *cooperate*, that is, to yield our lives to Him through prayer and the Word. Only then can He show us what's truly important—and then grant us the power to live that way.

How might we cooperate with God in this process? Let's begin by going to God's Word. In the book of 2 Thessalonians, writing to both those who follow God's way and those who don't, the apostle Paul had this to say: "We hear that some of you are living idle lives, refusing to work and wasting time meddling in other people's business. In the name of the Lord Jesus Christ, we appeal to such people—no, we command them: Settle down and get to work. Earn your own living. And I say to the rest of you, dear brothers and sisters, never get tired of doing good" (3:11–13 NLT).

In this passage Paul gave both a slap on the hand and an encouraging pat on the shoulder. There were people, he said, who were wasting time, and there were also those who were making good choices with their time. The same is true today. To the former, he says, settle down and work. To the latter, he says to never get tired of doing good.

There are three particular phrases in this passage that I'd like to give a little extra thought to. Looking at these three phrases will help us cooperate with God in this process of knowing what's truly valuable.

The phrases are (1) *We hear that some of you*, (2) *are living idle lives*, and (3) *never get tired of doing good*.

We hear that some of you . . .

What are people hearing about your life? Are you currently living in a way that's worthy of other people talking?

Now, I'm not suggesting that you should go brag about yourself so people will be talking. And the emphasis in life should never be building a spotless reputation or promoting your good deeds. But if someone were writing to someone else about you, what would he say? "I hear you're going after what matters most"? Or, "I hear you're not using your time wisely"? It's a great question to ask.

. . . are living idle lives

At first glance, most of us probably do not think the phrase "idle lives" applies to us. It's not possible in this Internet-fueled day and age, right? We're busy. We're movers and shakers. We have the moves and the grooves and the skills to pay the bills. Idle lives? Are you kidding me?!

But activity—even a lot of activity—is not the same as valuable activity. The question this phrase raises for us is, are all my moves really important? Just because you're busy doesn't mean you're busy with what matters most.

The word *idle* is a little confusing because it would seem to refer to not doing anything. But the opposite of idleness is not busyness. In another translation of this same verse the concept of idleness is expressed in the word *busybodies*—"I hear some of you . . . are busybodies" (NIV). *Busybodies* implies a lot of movement but no substance. The wheels are spinning, but nothing is moving. People are busy, just not with what matters most.

Do you know any busybodies? Let's get more personal. In a moment of honest reflection, could that describe *you*? Either you're trying to give the illusion of busyness, or you're legitimately busy. But are you really putting your time into what matters most? Are you pursuing the values you'd pursue if you knew death was right around the corner?

. . . never get tired of doing good

In adding this phrase, the apostle Paul wanted to make sure that those who were already doing good, and focusing on what matters most, didn't tire of doing good. He saw a danger that his readers would grow weary and become indifferent to living life to its fullest, and he didn't want them to be tempted to take the busybody route.

God doesn't either, and so His Word, spoken through Paul, is still relevant for readers today. It can speak to us in the same way that it spoke to people in the first century AD. To some, this passage can be a warning: *Don't waste your life being busy for what doesn't matter.* For others, the passage is saying, *Please don't tire of living God's way. Live like you have something to live for. Actually, live like you are dying . . . then you'll really be living.* Think about that: if we were to live as though we're dying, we would all experience increased clarity on what matters most, how to prioritize our time, and how to seize each day.

Let's talk about what this looks like in everyday life. Let me suggest two actions we can take to align our value system with God's.

Determine to Live with Passion

God is passionate. In fact, everything He ever does, He does with passion. And if we are going to live our lives in a way that reflects Him and adds value to others, then passion is worthy of our pursuit.

Passion goes deeper than excitement. I can get excited about a Diet Coke and a hot dog at a ball game. Excitement comes and goes. But passion bubbles up from our souls. It's what we live for most. It's what gets us up in the morning and keeps us going strong each day.

What's the bigger picture of passion? When we have passion, we recognize that life is short and it's meant to be lived largely, because we won't pass this way again. When we combine that recognition with God's bigger picture, we take it a step further and embrace eternal life over this temporal life. As we choose to follow God, our souls come alive, and He shows us that life is best lived when it's given away. He gives our passion a fresh start.

If we don't have passion, it can be a challenge to get. It's not like we can wake up in the morning and say, "I'm going to be passionate today. I'm going to turn on my Tony Robbins tapes, walk on hot coals, follow my bliss, and talk to people like I'm amped up on a triple espresso while pumping my fists." To gain passion, we must both choose it and pray that God will develop it within us. I like to say that passion "wakes up" as we yield our lives to God and begin to understand what matters most in life. And passion develops as we pursue what matters most. So here's an important question for you: are you living with passion? As you take an honest assessment of your life, is *passionate* a word that can aptly describe it?

If not, let's do some work in this area. To define what matters most, we have to get very practical. Let's break it down into a one-month-sized chunk. If you had one month to live, what would your values be? When you take the time to actually list them, it's very helpful in the management of your time. You'll know what to passionately pursue.

Personally, what would I do if I had one month to live?

First off, I'd want to make sure that the month wasn't February. I'd want those extra two to three days the other months give. Then I'd make my list. I'd write down everything I would want to do. Undoubtedly on that list would be some unrealistic things that I would quickly find I couldn't *really* incorporate into the rest of my life (which is the purpose of making this list in the first place). For instance, I couldn't feasibly eat Ben & Jerry's ice cream every hour of my life. Maybe I could do that if I only had one month to live, but I surely couldn't get away with it for the next forty years or so. I couldn't feasibly quit my job either. I'm not sure I would want to, even if I only had thirty remaining days of life. But I'd definitely cut down on answering e-mail and attend fewer meetings at church.

On my list would be things like "Give full attention to my family." That's good, but it's kind of broad. Nothing becomes motivating until it becomes specific. So, with each action on my list, I would ask a follow-up question: how can I *specifically* pursue these values within my current lifestyle? (My current lifestyle is as a workingman/husband/father of three teenagers—that life stage is technically called "UBER-FUL.") Whether you're single, college age, an empty nester, whatever, you can ask the same question. Then do some specific analysis.

For instance, on my list, when I wrote down, "Give full attention to my family," I followed it with four specific actions to help fulfill that pursuit:

1. Ask follow-up questions each time they answer me. I have to do a better job of shutting off my own internal dialogue and really listen instead.

2. Don't talk on the phone when anyone from my family is in the car.

3. With Cathy, choose conversation with her over relaxation for me. I know my wife is different from most women (just kidding), but she likes to talk. To me. About "stuff." I don't get it always . . . but, whatever.

4. Say yes to all "Dad, do you want to . . . ?" questions (e.g., "Dad, do you want to play catch?" "Dad, do you want to go to the pool?" "Dad, do you want to go to another room and leave me and my friends alone?").

Once I identified specific actions to fulfill, I moved to another question: what might need to change so I can achieve these constantly?

Let's pick the one about the phone in the car. A few years ago I gave an example in a sermon about how mobile phones are stealing valuable time today from significant relationships. You would have thought I was asking for money to buy guns for Iraqi children—that comment created a lot of squirming in our congregation. But I guarantee that if you had thirty days to live, you wouldn't be taking valuable time away from your family members on trivial phone conversations about the e-mail server being down or whatever.

So, if that makes your list, what might need to change? You might need to turn off the phone when you get in the car with family members. I am not the expert here, but I read in the *Wall Street Journal* that most modern phones do indeed have an Off button. Or you may need to leave that ridiculous-looking Mr. Spock earpiece out of your ear when you're with your family. Some of you even shower and sleep with it in. Hey—give it a rest already. You used to make fun of others wearing it; now you're one of them. You Bluetooth sellout, you!

Answering these questions honestly will take some work. But the questions will help guide you on how to spend your most valuable currency—time. Take a few minutes and think through the questions that follow. Write your answers in the spaces provided. If you need more space, write them in a notebook or journal instead.

» *If I had one month to live, what would I value most?*

_____

_____

_____

_____

» *How can I specifically pursue these values within my current lifestyle?*

_____

_____

_____

_____

» *What might need to change so I can achieve these constantly?*

_____

_____

_____

_____

That's how passion is created!

A second action we can take to align our value system with God's values and cooperate with Him in the process of living them out, is this: *Depend on God!*

Depend on God's Power to Help You Live Out the Right Values

If you've ever been to a funeral, I'm pretty sure you've informally gone through the following process: You sit quietly in the funeral service and grieve the loss of a life, and in that quietness you resolve to sharpen your goals. The reality of death awakens something in you, and in that moment you want to focus on what really matters most. Maybe you go home and change the way you treat your close friends or family. That happens often for a day or two. Then that resolve fades. Why?

Easy answer! It fades because you go back to relying on your own willpower rather than on God's power. I know this because I've gone through this spiritual ping-pong match many times myself. And my willpower isn't enough for what matters most.

To be successful at this, we must move from willpower to real power. This is where I depend on God to help me define and achieve what matters most. It relates to all areas we've talked about in this book, and more, including time management, key relationships, finances, career, dating and marriage, and behaviors and attitudes of the heart.

For me, a critical transformation took place when I realized that I had all of God's power available to me. Romans 8:11 explains this for us: "If the Spirit of him who raised Jesus from the dead is living in you, he who raised Christ from the dead will also give life to your mortal bodies through his Spirit, who lives in you." This means that, as a Christian, since I have the Holy Spirit in my life, I have access to His power. The same power that was available to Jesus is available to me too! That's power to heal relationships, work in my family and on the job, rescue my life when I need it, and help me focus on what matters most. His power is available to you as well. He'll help you live the life you were created to live. God will give you all the power you need to get a fresh start. He will help you make up for lost time as you finally begin to pursue what matters most!

Another Scripture passage that helps put this into perspective is Ephesians 1:19–20. Paul wrote, "I pray that you will begin to understand the incredible greatness of his power for us who believe in him. This is the same mighty power that raised Christ from the dead and seated him in the place of honor at God's right hand in the heavenly realms" (NLT).

The same power that defeated death on Easter morning! The same power that created this incredible playground we call earth! This *same power* is available to *you*, to help you live a life with meaning!

But there is a condition to obtaining this power. Did you notice it in the verse from Romans? It says, "If the spirit of him who raised Jesus from the dead is *living in you* . . ." This power is available *only* to those who believe. If you're not a believer, this might sound like bad news. But it can easily be changed to good news if you believe in Jesus and put your faith in Him. All you have to do is say yes to Him today. Are you familiar with that famous verse, John 3:16? It says that God loved the world so much that He gave his Son Jesus to die for us, and that if we *believe* in Him, God gives us eternal life. That's the foundation of being a Christian. It's also the foundation of a fresh start—and it's available to you right now.

Your Fresh Start Today

When you understand the temporal nature of life, it will keep you focused on what matters most. It's not about adding years to your life; it's about adding life to your years. How *do* we add life to our years? By pulling free from everything that keeps us stuck in a place where spiritual growth is unattainable. That's what we've aimed to focus on in this book. There are so many things in life that can get us stuck; we've looked at several of them. But I hope that by now you know there *is* a way out. Christ invites us to move forward into abundant new life.

Do you remember, back in chapter 1, the scripture I quoted from the book of Isaiah? If not, let me refresh your memory: "I am about to do something new. See, I have already begun! Do you not see it? I will make a pathway through the wilderness. I will create rivers in the dry wasteland" (Isaiah 43:19 NLT). *Rivers!* Not swamps, filled with life-strangling, dream-stifling muck, but flowing *rivers*.

And isn't that what you want today? To get out of the mud and take a cool, refreshing swim in the river of abundant life? Then do it! Jump in! You don't have to be stuck any longer. You've been handed a new lease on life—a God-given *fresh start*.

And it begins today!

JOURNAL AND SMALL GROUP GUIDE

Most everyone I know who reads a book usually feels a sense of accomplishment after finishing it. I know I do. So, first of all, congratulations! Secondly, some of what you just read requires deep, heart-penetrating reflection and dialogue. A next step toward a true fresh start is to wrestle with this material. There are several ways to do this, but the two that resonate with how I'm wired are to (1) share my thoughts with the friends in my small group, and (2) write thoughts in my journal. The following questions will work for both formats. If you're currently unconnected to a small group, consider asking a friend or two to read along with you and help you process the questions as you finish a chapter. You'll have a richer experience, and it will result in deeper friendships. It's a gift to have time to think and reflect and discuss . . . my prayer is that you'll open that gift.

Blessings, Doug

CHAPTER ONE:
UNSTUCK

Reflect and discuss

1. What are the areas in which you feel you are most stuck and most need a fresh start?

2. What kind of change do you really desire for your life?

3. Jesus promised an abundant life (John 10:10). In your opinion, what does an abundant life look like? Does this match up with the changes you desire?

Journal and go personal

1. Spend a few moments thinking about God's work in your life. Describe a time when He showed up big-time and created personal renewal. When you're discouraged, how can this give you hope?

2. What are some practical ways you can let go of control and cooperate with God's work to sanctify your life? Describe your idea of a sanctified solution to your "stuck" problems.

CHAPTER TWO:
PRIDE vs. GOD-SIZED DREAMS

Reflect and discuss

1. What were some of your childhood dreams?

2. How does it make you feel to think about laying down your dreams? What is your first reaction to that thought?

3. In light of your answers, what is your response to Christ's humility?

Journal and go personal

1. Take some time to consider and write about some of your current dreams. Beneath the surface, do any of them revolve around selfishness?

2. How does pride most often show up in your life? What are some practical ways you could be more humble in your interactions with others this week?

CHAPTER THREE:
THE STRANGE INGREDIENT OF SUCCESS

Reflect and discuss

1. What is your current idea of success? How has that changed over the years?

2. What tends to keep you from having an attitude that leads to serving? Do you have typical excuses you use to rationalize your way out of it?

3. What are some opportunities for service that seem to keep coming your way? If you've been avoiding them, why do think that is? How can you keep from missing them?

Journal and go personal

1. Who are some people in your life you could serve? Write a list of a few small acts of service you can do today or tomorrow.

2. Write out a personal prayer to God, asking Him to transform your heart to become more like Jesus' in the area of service. Continue to pray it this week.

CHAPTER FOUR:
BEYOND YOUR PAST

Reflect and discuss

1. Reflect on your own conversion. In that moment, what did you *hope* you would break free from?

2. Name your guilt. Which one do you relate to most: guilt that separates from salvation, service, or intimacy (page 52)?

3. In this chapter there were four common areas where people choose the world's way rather than God's way: money, sex, relationships (friends and family), and work ethic (page 48). Which of these do you struggle with most? Which do you struggle with the least? How do you normally rationalize the "little sins" in your life?

Journal and go personal

1. Can you think of some people who would be helped by your story of a transformed life? Who would those people be, and how might you take steps to communicate your story to them?

2. What would your life look like if you had zero guilt, shame, or regret? What's keeping you from receiving the joy that comes with God's forgiveness? Pray this week for God to remove those hang-ups from your life.

CHAPTER FIVE:
FREEDOM FROM HURT

Reflect and discuss

1. Whom do you need to forgive? Where are you on the forgiveness checklist mentioned on page 74?

2. What are some triggers in your life that cause you to relive pain and rehearse the tale of being wronged?

3. What are some practical steps you could take to make forgiveness a regular part of your life?

Journal and go personal

1. Do you have someone or some people in your life you can't imagine loving? Who are they? Write out a plan to start praying for them this week.

2. How do you feel about God stamping "paid in full" on your life (page 71)? Why is there a connection between God's grace for you and your ability to "release the offender"?

CHAPTER SIX:
CONFLICT: AN UNIMAGINED ADVENTURE

Reflect and discuss

1. What is your typical response to a conflict with someone you are close to? Do you grow angry? Stew? Deny the conflict? Swipe silently (page 85)?

2. What are some parts of your natural response that might be considered healthy? What are some parts that are unhealthy?

3. In what ways would facing an upcoming conflict give you opportunities to trust God?

Journal and go personal

1. What would it look like for you to get angry and not sin; to get angry in a way that's healthy and good? Think of an instance of past anger to help you compare.

2. Consider a recent conflict and work through the steps described beginning on page 84 (*Ouch!—What?—Who?—What?*).

CHAPTER SEVEN:
TO BOLDLY GO

Reflect and discuss

1. Where does discouragement show up in your life? What kinds of things regularly discourage you most?

2. How could you change your scenery? Who might you need to space yourself from? What expectation(s) might you need to change?

3. When you were last discouraged, what do you think God was trying to teach you about Himself? Were there any areas you needed to change in *your*self?

Journal and go personal

1. Can you see a cycle of discouragement in your life? Take a few minutes to identify and write about it so you are prepared to avoid it next time it comes around.

2. Who is someone you could encourage? How might you start? Make a plan this week and put it into action.

CHAPTER EIGHT:
BETTER TOGETHER

Reflect and discuss

1. When you hear "better together," who in your life do you think about? To whom are you "known"?

2. What scares you about a deep friendship?

3. Are you typically an encouraging person? What would the people around you say? How can you be more intentional about encouraging others?

Journal and go personal

1. Trust, transparency, and beauty are three characteristics of deep friendships. When it comes to your closest friends, how are these expressed? What are some ways you can develop these characteristics in your relationships?

2. Think about your life and a few people you might be able to reach out and connect with. Who are those people? How can you take the first steps? Who can hold you accountable?

CHAPTER NINE:
REDEEMED REJECTION

Reflect and discuss

1. In what ways does the fear of rejection impact your relationships with your coworkers and close friends?

2. Where do you currently feel the sting of rejection most? Professional, physical, parental, rejection from your kids, recreational, athletic, dating, marital, spiritual (page 127)?

3. Who has rejected or is rejecting you? To whom do you need to offer compassion?

Journal and go personal

1. Describe a desired fresh start (over rejection) as a result of feeling and expressing compassion.

2. What are some practical, personal, and healthy ways you might begin to care less about what others think?

CHAPTER TEN:
ANALYZED ANGER

Reflect and discuss

1. What emotion typically makes you the most angry? What's your usual response?

2. What are some things that regularly trigger your anger? Pick a time in the recent past when you got angry and go deeper: what might have been at the root of your anger?

3. Which one of the practical ways of defusing anger (page 156) can you see yourself practicing in the future?

Journal and go personal

1. Think about something that may (or probably will) make you angry this week. What is something you could do to delay and diffuse your response?

2. Anger is okay! (Ps. 4:4; Eph. 4:26.) What significance might this have for you personally?

CHAPTER ELEVEN:
SHARING YOUR FRESH-START STORY

Reflect and discuss

1. In your life, what connection have you seen between knowing God and talking about him with others?

2. Who is someone you could care for spiritually? How can you start a conversation about Jesus? What is your common ground?

3. Consider your attitude and thoughts about the non-believers you know: are you more accepting or more judgmental? What are the kinds of things you judge quickly? Go beneath the surface: what's really motivating your reaction to them?

Journal and go personal

1. Do you know your spiritual story? Write out how you would tell someone about the impact God has had on your life.

2. What did you learn from the woman at the well and her conversation with Jesus (page 165)? How were you challenged and/or encouraged?

CHAPTER TWELVE:
WHAT YOU VALUE MOST

Reflect and discuss

1. What do you value most?

2. What percentage of your time do you think you spend on what you value most? Is that enough time? Explain.

3. How are you challenged by the following verses: James 4:14; Ps. 90:12; and 2 Thess. 3:11–13 (pages 182 and 183)?

Journal and go personal

1. Write out a list of what you value and desire to passionately pursue so you can return to it often. How might returning to this list help you? Is it worth the hassle?

2. What does tomorrow look like in light of your fresh start? What are some immediate changes you need to make? What are some conversations you need to have? Who can help keep you accountable?

NOTES

Introduction

1. Story and quote in David Jeremiah, "Not Too Old," *Turning Points Magazine* 10, no. 6 (July 2008): 45.

Chapter 2

1. C. S. Lewis, *Mere Christianity* (1952; repr. New York: HarperCollins, 2001), 121–22, 124. Citations are to the 2001 edition.

Chapter 4

1. Wikiquote, http://en.wikiquote.org/wiki/The_Lion_King.

Chapter 6

1. I'm being general with this illustration because I don't want to identify one of my three children.

Chapter 10

1. Dietrich Bonhoeffer, *Life Together: The Classic Exploration of Faith in Community* (New York: Harper & Row, 1954; repr., San Francisco: HarperOne, 1978), 110.
2. *Merriam Webster's Collegiate Dictionary*, 11th ed., s.v., "defuse."

Chapter 11

1. Frank Newport, "Belief in God Far Lower in Western U.S.," Gallup, 28 July 2008, http://www.gallup.com/poll/109108/Belief-God-Far-Lower-Western-US.aspx.
2. Ibid., "Questions and Answers about America's Religions: More than 8 out of 10 Americans Identify with a Christian Faith," Gallup, 24 December 2007, http://www.gallup.com/poll/103459/Questions-Answers-About-Americans-Religion.aspx.

ACKNOWLEDGMENTS

Although there is one name on the cover of this book, there are literally thousands of people who have cheered me on through prayer and encouragement at Saddleback Church, who challenge me to write out what I get to teach. For almost twenty years, Saddleback has been a place where I get to think about God's Word and teach it to hungry people, young and old, who want to live out God's ways with passion. I deeply love our church body! Thank you for your love for me and your constant affirmation of my gifts.

Specific names that are beyond worthy to be mentioned here are two of my anchors and bookends in life, who help me in so many ways: Matt McGill and Jana Sarti. Thank you two for reading every word and helping me with the questions in the back of the book, but most of all thanks for just being dear friends and coworkers in Kingdom work. I'm also indebted to several others who played various roles in my life during the writing of this book and helped make *Fresh Start* a reality: Brian Bird; Marcus Brotherton; Allison Hibbard; Jason Pogue; and my buddy Holden at Fuddruckers for always having an open booth, a gracious greeting and a good meal when I came into write. Also, thanks to Greg Johnson, my agent at WordServeLiterary.com for pushing me and believing in me more than I believe in myself—you are a good man (even though I'm not a big enough name to be on your Web site). Thanks to the good folks at Thomas Nelson who are so easy to work with: Matt Baugher for trusting me and giving me a platform bigger than my youth ministry world—you are gracious. And to Renee Chavez for editing with passion, deep convictions, and a loose enough grip that allowed me to "win" most of the time. I so appreciate all the little extras that you added to the manuscript—you are a real pro and made this a better book than I could have written on my own. And thank you, Jennifer McNeil, for overseeing the whole project in such a pleasant and professional way—if there are better teams out there than Thomas Nelson I'd like to meet them.

Finally, no words of thanks are big enough to cover the grace of my family—especially my in-laws. I've written dozens of books and I'm not sure I've ever mentioned them . . . uh, sorry. Jack and Patricia Guiso you are two of the greatest humans on the planet, the most supportive in-laws, and the best grandparents anyone could ever ask for. You are a gift to me personally and a bright spot with our kids—they love and adore you. Torie, Cody, and Cassie Fields, as always my love for you is indescribable—the only thing I really want to be known for is being a good and loving dad. You are always on my mind, and nothing can make me cry like thinking about my love for you and the fact that I get to be your earthly father. Finally, "thanks" seems too trivial for my bride Cathy . . . but thank you, babe, for supporting me through this! I wish the world could capture what I get to see in you! Although you don't write or speak to crowds, you have so much to say about life, love, faith, Jesus, friendship, depth, fresh starts, and intimacy. While I'm writing and speaking about it, you are living it out in such a way that I know God is pleased. What a gift you are to me, our family, your friends, and our world. I love you deeply.

ABOUT THE AUTHOR

Doug Fields has been one of the teaching pastors at Saddleback Community Church in Mission Viejo, California, since 1992. He has authored or coauthored more than 50 books, including the recently released *Refuel: An Uncomplicated Way to Connect with God*. His highly acclaimed, award-winning book *Purpose Driven Youth Ministry* has helped shape the course of youth ministry worldwide.

Doug earned an MDiv from Fuller Theological Seminary, and a BA from Vanguard University. He and his wife, Cathy, have three children and live in Southern California.

+

IF YOU'VE ALWAYS STRUGGLED WITH THE STEREOTYPICAL QUIET TIME,
DON'T GIVE UP HOPE!

As a Christian, you know you need to have devotions. You've heard it from your pastor; you've seen the study guides; you may have even made a dent in the One Year Bible. Some of you have valiantly set your alarm clocks back an hour for morning quiet time, only to find that life creeps back in to steal your resolve. It isn't because you don't love God. You quit because you "bought into" someone's unsustainable habit at an unreasonable pace.

But you don't have to keep running on empty. Bestselling author Doug Fields offers an uncomplicated, practical plan that you *can* carry out. This book won't teach you how to "cram God" into your already full schedule. Instead, Doug will show you a practical, doable way of setting God first, and then letting everything else in your life fall into place. You will experience the fullness God has for you—just take some time to refuel.

Now available wherever books are sold!

—

THOMAS NELSON
Since 1798